Canada's

Income

Security

Programs

by Christopher Clark

Canadian Council on Social Development

Canadian Cataloguing in Publication Data

Clark, Christopher J., 1969–
        Canada's income security programs

Issued also in French under title: Les programmes de sécurité du revenu au
        Canada.
Includes bibliographical references.
ISBN 0-88810-463-4

        1. Income maintenance programs--Canada. 2. Social security--Canada.
        I. Canadian Council on Social Development. II. Title.

HD7129.C52 1998   368.4'00971   C98-900363-9

Printed and bound in Canada by Ottawa Select Printing Inc.

Published by:
The Canadian Council on Social Development
441 MacLaren, 4th Floor
Ottawa, Ontario K2P 2H3
Tel: (613) 236-8977; fax: (613) 236-2750
Email: council@ccsd.ca   Internet: www.ccsd.ca

Table of Contents

List of Tables

Foreword

Since 1920, the Canadian Council on Social Development (CCSD) has produced fact books and reports to help Canadians understand the different dimensions of their economic and social security systems. Over the last several years, we have published reports on the following subjects: the labour market's effectiveness in generating adequate incomes; the gender gap in earnings; how Canadians are preparing for and adjusting to retirement; urban poverty; the progress of children; the consequences of child poverty; and, since 1975, the CCSD has produced the standard reference authority on poverty in Canada. All these reports and fact books focus on the conditions that give rise to the state of our social fabric and the need for social protection.

Canada's Income Security Programs takes a slightly different approach. It provides Canadians with a condensed description, in popular language, of an important group of programs that were created to respond to these needs for social protection in a number of areas. It is these programs that have become the backbone of our public social security system in Canada.

Until the 1960s, income security programs were neither too numerous nor too complex for the general public to comprehend. Since then, however, the number of programs has expanded considerably, and a movement beginning in the 1970s to target programs to particular groups of recipients and to integrate many of them into the tax system has made the programs more selective and largely incomprehensible to most people.

In this book, Christopher Clark has not only provided accurate descriptions of our current income security programs, but also brief histories of each. He describes programs such as the National Child Benefit that provides benefits to families; social assistance and GST credits that provide assistance to households; programs like (un)employment insurance and CPP/QPP disability and workers' compensation that provide earnings replacement based on social insurance principles; and retirement programs such as Old Age Security, the new Seniors Benefit, and RRSPs.

The book concludes with an innovative examination of who benefits from these programs. Many readers will be surprised to learn that Canada's income security programs offer protection to a wide range of Canadians at different income levels. Perhaps that is why they are valued so highly.

Canada's Income Security Programs will be a useful companion to the valuable and detailed inventory of programs published by Human Resources Development Canada.

David P. Ross
CCSD Executive Director

Acknowledgements

I would like to thank the many people who contributed their time and advice throughout the process of writing this book. Thanks specifically to individuals in the following departments who reviewed the text: Human Resources Development Canada in the Social Policy Information and Analysis Division, the Income Security Branch, and the Employment Insurance Branch; the Department of Finance; Veterans' Affairs Canada; Régie des Rentes du Québec; and provincial and territorial ministries of income security and social services. People from a number of non-governmental organizations also provided substantial input, including individuals from the Association of Workers' Compensation Boards of Canada, the Canadian Labour Congress, the National Anti-Poverty Organization, and the National Council of Welfare.

Many CCSD staff members also contributed greatly to this book. First and foremost, I would like to thank Clarence Lochhead who co-authored the book's final chapter. Others at the CCSD who made a significant contribution include: Executive Director David Ross; former CCSD research associate Richard Shillington; research assistant Spyridoula Tsoukalas; and Ellen Adelberg, Doreen Lint, Nancy Perkins, and Arlette Sinquin of the CCSD's Communications Department.

This book is dedicated to my wife, Andrée, whose support and advice are unparalleled.

Introduction

The purpose of this book is to provide readers with a comprehensive and easy-to-read description of Canada's income security programs. It is a basic reference tool for anyone – from the casual reader, to the student of politics or public policy, to policy analysts, researchers, and policy-makers. In short, it is for anyone who has an interest in income security programs. *Canada's Income Security Programs* is organized so that infor-mation can be quickly located, digested, and used to support a range of needs.

Chapters 1 through 4 each begin by outlining the historical evolution of the income security programs covered in that chapter. These brief historical reviews provide the reader with an understanding of how and why the various programs were put into place. From this base of knowledge, the reader moves on to more detailed descriptions of each of the programs as they are currently designed, including comprehensive descriptions of the following: what the particular program is and what it is intended to do; the benefits available and how people qualify for these benefits; and, the number of people that receive support and the value of individual and total benefits paid. In Chapter 5, each of Canada's major income security programs is re-examined in relation to its impact on the incomes of Canadians, and the role of each program for different types of households is analysed.

Chapter 1 examines the development and current status of child benefit programs in Canada. After tracing the evolution of such programs – from a tax exemption for families with children in 1919 to the establishment of the Child Tax Benefit in 1993 – the current system of both federal and provincial child benefit programs is described in detail. The new Canada Child Tax Benefit and federal-provincial efforts to establish a National

Child Benefits System are outlined, as are federal tax provisions such as the Child Care Expense Deduction and the Equivalent-to-Spouse Credit, and numerous provincial benefits and tax provisions for families with children.

Chapter 2 provides a description of social assistance and other income supports, then and now, from the range of basic supports established over the course of the Great Depression and two World Wars, to a national system of provincially administered supports under the Canada Assistance Plan in the 1960s. The current provincial social assistance programs and the most recent trends in the administration of benefits are described, along with a comparison of provincial and territorial benefit levels. This chapter also examines the income security benefits and special tax supports available to persons with disabilities and war veterans.

Chapter 3 focuses on the two major programs that provide a replacement for lost earnings: federal Employment Insurance (previously called Unemployment Insurance) and provincial Workers' Compensation. This chapter traces the history of the Unemployment Insurance program from its meagre beginnings in 1941, the expansions in the 1960s and 1970s, to the contractions of the 1980s and 1990s. This is followed by a full description of the new Employment Insurance system that took effect in January 1996. The second part of the chapter describes the development of Workers' Compensation in Canada and highlights the main components of these provincially based programs.

Chapter 4 guides readers through the complex system of supports in Canada's retirement income system. Three sections describe the development and current status of the old age security system, the Canada and Quebec Pension Plans, and tax-assisted private pension and retirement savings plans. Details about the proposed Seniors Benefit are also provided, along with recent changes to the Canada and Quebec Pension Plans, and tax provisions for Registered Retirement Savings Plans.

Chapter 5 differs from the earlier chapters. Rather than examining the evolution of specific programs and their current structures, this chapter pulls together each of Canada's major income security programs and examines its impact on the incomes of Canadians. Within this analysis, the differing roles of social insurance and basic income support programs are examined, as is the impact of these programs on different types of households including families with children, the elderly, and households at various income levels.

A glossary is provided for terms commonly used in the income security field. Terms such as "benefit indexation," "equalization," and "claw-back" are explained and placed into context for the reader.

It is important to note that the information in this book is based on the most accurate and current data available as of the end of 1997. Governments at all levels periodically introduce small changes to programs, and sometimes they even undertake large-scale reforms of a particular program or income tax provision. As this book went to print early in 1998, several small changes were announced or had just taken effect. These changes – including a number of measures identified in the 1998 federal budget – are outlined in Appendix 1.

Chapter 1
Child Benefits

Background

Child benefits have existed in Canada for as long as the income tax system.[1] In 1919, following the establishment of federal income taxes, the federal government introduced a tax exemption for families with children. There were substantial national debates over this measure throughout the 1920s and 1930s, with opposing views expressed about whether or not direct income supports for families with children – then referred to as "family allowances" – were also required. Despite widespread discussions, no consensus or changes to the family tax exemption emerged during this period.

The issue of family allowances resurfaced in the first half of the 1940s. In 1945, the federal government introduced a universal Family Allowance program which paid benefits to every family with children in the country. The federal Family Allowance program represented one of the pillars of the new welfare state in Canada, and it received broad public support for several decades. An example of this support was the ill-fated attempt by the federal government in 1972 to replace the universal Family Allowance program with an income-tested program called the Family Income Security Plan that would be available only to low- and middle-income families. Public pressure to maintain a universal allowance caused the government to abandon its plans.

1

The 1970s witnessed a number of changes to child benefits in Canada. In 1972, the federal government introduced the Child Care Expense Deduction to assist some families with the costs of child care. In 1973, the Family Allowance was tripled in value, made taxable, and indexed to the cost of living. Several years later, in 1978, the federal government introduced a tax credit targeted specifically at low- and middle-income families with children – the Refundable Child Tax Credit. This new credit was financed through reductions in Family Allowances and several other long-standing universal tax supports for families with children. The net result was a substantial increase in benefits for low- and middle-income families and a reduction in support for higher-income families.

Increased targeting and the reduction of child-related benefits continued in the 1980s. It was during this period that the federal government changed the tax exemption for families with children (first established in 1919) into a non-refundable credit. In 1985, inflation protection for Family Allowances was weakened by having the allowances indexed only partially, rather than fully, to changes in the inflation rate. In 1989, the non-refundable and refundable child tax credits were also reduced from full to partial indexation. Starting in 1989, a special "claw-back" on Family Allowances – a separate tax on the benefits – was phased in over three years so that the benefits were fully recovered from high-income families.

Throughout the 1970s and 1980s, several provinces also introduced child benefits of their own.[2] Governments in Saskatchewan, Manitoba, and Quebec each put in place a combination of family allowances or income supplements for low-income families with children. Saskatchewan's Family Income Plan (1974), Manitoba's Child Related Income Support Program (1981), Quebec's Family Allowance Program (1974), Quebec's Allowance for Young Children (1989), and Quebec's Allowance for Newborn Children (1988) provided benefits to low-income families with children, regardless of their source(s) of income. Quebec also introduced the Work Income

2

Supplement Program (1979) and later, the Parental Wage Assistance Program in 1988 – which replaced the 1979 program – to supplement the employment earnings of low-income families with children.

The targeting mantra of the late 1970s and 1980s persisted into the 1990s, as the federal government continued to shift the balance of child benefits to lower-income families. In 1993, the federal Family Allowance and the refundable and non-refundable child tax credits were replaced with a single income-tested benefit – the Child Tax Benefit. Recipients of the Child Tax Benefit who had employment earnings were also eligible for a new child benefit called the Working Income Supplement.

The Current Child Benefits System

The current child benefits system in Canada is comprised of a range of federal benefits for families with children including the Child Tax Benefit and Working Income Supplement, the Child Care Expense Deduction, the Equivalent-to-Spouse Credit, maternity/parental benefits under Employment Insurance (see Chapter 3), and orphan's and children's benefits under the Canada Pension Plan (see Chapter 4), as well as a host of provincial benefits. This combination of federal and provincial benefits is intended to recognize the costs associated with, and the societal value of, raising children.

The Child Tax Benefit and Working Income Supplement

The Child Tax Benefit (CTB) is a tax-free monthly benefit paid by the federal government to eligible families with children in Canada.[3] Some CTB recipients with earnings are also eligible for the Working Income Supplement. In 1996, the federal government spent $5.1 billion on the Child Tax Benefit and Working Income Supplement.[4]

To be eligible for the Child Tax Benefit, an applicant must be primarily responsible for raising a child under the age of 18. In general, it is the mother of the child that meets this criteria, but it can also be the father, a grandparent, or a legal guardian of the child. The CTB applicant must live with the child and be a resident of Canada.[5] Applications for the CTB are made to Revenue Canada.[6]

Although the vast majority (80 per cent) of families with children under the age of 18 receive the Child Tax Benefit, only those with incomes[7] of less than $25,921 were eligible for the maximum benefit in 1997. The maximum CTB is reduced gradually until it disappears when family income reaches an upper limit ($66,721 in 1997) for one- and two-child families. Payment levels are based on the number of children in a family, and the family's previous year's income reported at tax time. Benefit adjustments related to changes in family income occur in July of each year.

The maximum Child Tax Benefit was $85 per month per child in 1997 (or $1,020 per year), plus $6 per month ($75 per year) for a third and each subsequent child. Families that do not claim the Child Care Expense Deduction are eligible for an additional amount ($18 per month or $213 per year in 1997) for each child under the age of seven.[8] These amounts are indexed to any amount of inflation that rises above three per cent per year. Different CTB rates have been established in Alberta and Quebec, where the provincial governments have taken up a federal provision that enables them to tailor the program to their province's needs. In Alberta, CTB rates vary according to the age of the child. In Quebec, the CTB varies according to the age *and* rank of the child.[9]

Some families with employment earnings are also eligible for the Working Income Supplement (WIS). In 1997, the WIS started once family earnings[10] reached $3,750, and rose until a maximum level of earnings was reached.[11] The maximum Working Income Supplement in 1997 was paid to families with annual incomes between $10,000 and $20,921, after which benefits declined and eventually disappeared once family income exceeded $25,921.[12] The maximum WIS in 1997 was $50 a month ($605 a year) for the first child, $34 a month ($405 a year) for the second child, and $28 a month ($330 a year) for each additional child.[13] Prior to July 1997, the WIS was paid on a family basis, rather than per child. The annual maximum was $500 per family.

The Proposed National Child Benefits System

In its 1997 budget, the federal government proposed that the Child Tax Benefit be combined with the Working Income Supplement to form a new Canada Child Tax Benefit (CCTB) that would take effect in July 1998.[14] As part of the new proposal, the federal government made a commitment to improve benefits and increase the combined CTB/WIS spending from the 1996 level of $5.1 billion to almost $6 billion in 1998.[15] The July 1997 improvements to the Working Income Supplement accounted for $250 million of the approximately $850 million proposed increase. The federal government has since promised to spend an additional $850 million to further enhance the Canada Child Tax Benefit, once it is fully implemented.

The proposed merger of the Child Tax Benefit and Working Income Supplement has been billed as the "foundation" for a new National Child Benefits System. Under this new system, the federal government would provide a base benefit – the new Canada Child Tax Benefit – to all low- and modest-income families with children in Canada, regardless of their source(s) of income.[16] This federal income assistance would be supplemented by a combination of provincial/territorial income

5

and service supports for low-income families with children. The province of Quebec is not participating in this new national initiative, but has stated that it supports the principles of the plan. Instead, Quebec has introduced its own child benefits system as part of a broader family policy (described later in this chapter).

A major impetus behind the proposed National Child Benefits System is the growing public concern about the problem of child poverty in Canada. There is also a consensus emerging among the various levels of government that the current federal/provincial/territorial system of supports for low-income families does not encourage social assistance recipients to find employment and become self-sufficient. Governments have also shown an interest in improving supports for families that are poor despite their participation in the labour market – the so-called "working poor."

In explaining the rationale behind the proposed changes, a joint federal/provincial/territorial government document notes that low-income families with children, particularly those headed by single parents, are sometimes better off financially on provincial social assistance than they would be in a low-paying job.[17] That occurs because families that leave social assistance must give up a range of income supports (such as welfare benefits on behalf of their children) and "in-kind" supports (such as dental coverage and prescription drugs), while incurring new costs that are associated with working (such as child care, transportation, clothing expenses, and paying income and payroll taxes). The new National Child Benefits System would attempt to address this problem by separating income and in-kind supports that are administered from the welfare system on behalf of children, and extending them to *all* low-income families with children.

Despite the recent and proposed increases in federal child benefits, many recipients of the current Child Tax Benefit who rely primarily on social assistance for their income are not

6

expected to receive any additional income support. That is because as federal child benefits are increased, most provincial and territorial governments are expected to reduce their social assistance payments to families with children by a corresponding amount. At the very least, the provinces and territories have made a commitment that current recipients of the Child Tax Benefit will not be worse off as a result of the changes.

To ensure that any provincial and territorial savings that result from the increase in federal benefits are used to improve income and service supports for low-income families with children, the federal, provincial, and territorial governments have agreed to design a "re-investment framework" that is expected to be unveiled in 1998. This agreement will outline the areas of reinvestment that are considered appropriate, such as income-tested child benefits (including working-income supplements), child care, and dental and prescription drug coverage for low-income families with children.

Under the proposed Canada Child Tax Benefit, maximum benefits would be paid to *all* families with children and annual incomes below $20,921. The proposed maximums are as follows: $1,625 a year for families with one child; $3,050 for families with two children; $4,475 for families with three children; and, $5,900 for families with four children. These amounts mirror the benefits currently paid to families who are eligible for the maximums of both the Child Tax Benefit *and* the Working Income Supplement. However, since eligibility for the proposed integrated benefit would be wider than under the current combined CTB/WIS, federal funding for child benefits is projected to rise by about $600 million in July 1998.

Child Care Expense Deduction

The Child Care Expense Deduction[18] is intended to assist families that pay for child care.[19] The deduction is administered by Revenue Canada through the tax system. About 800,000 families claim the Child Care Expense Deduction.[20] For the 1996 tax year, it was estimated that this provision cost the federal government $335 million in foregone revenue and the provinces about another $194 million.[21]

Families can claim the Child Care Expense Deduction for each child under the age of 16. There is no age limit for dependants who require long-term care because of infirmities or disabilities. The applicant can be the child's parent, spouse of the parent, or a person caring for a dependant with a disability. In families headed by two adults, the lower-income spouse must make the application.

A claim for the Child Care Expense Deduction can be made if child care was required while the applicant was engaged in employment, education, or training-related activities.

> ### How the Child Care Deduction Works
>
> Jamie and Carolyn have two children, aged eight and four. As the applicant, Carolyn's potential maximum claim is $8,000, based on the number and ages of her children ($5,000 for the child under age seven and $3,000 for the child aged seven to 16). If this couple had spent at least $8,000 on child care expenses during the year, *and* if two-thirds of Carolyn's earned income was above $8,000, she could claim the full amount. However, if she incurred only $4,000 worth of child care expenses during the year, her maximum deduction would be $4,000, not $8,000.

Standard, licenced and unlicensed child-care arrangements qualify for the deduction, as do a number of other services such as summer or day camps and boarding schools. Only receipted expenses can be claimed.

The maximum deduction for the 1996 tax year was $5,000 for each child under the age of seven, and $3,000 for each child between the ages of seven and 16 and for dependants over the age of 16 with infirmities. Not all families are eligible to claim the maximum deduction. Applicants can only claim the *lesser* of: the combined value of the $5,000/$3,000 per-child maximums (for example, $10,000 for families with two children under the age of 7); two-thirds of the applicant's earned income;[22] or, the total value of the applicant's child care expenses. The maximum amounts are not indexed to inflation.

Since the benefit is in the form of a tax deduction and not a direct payment or credit, the actual value of the Child Care Expense Deduction to a recipient varies according to one's tax bracket. As a result, the deduction provides greater federal and provincial tax savings for higher-income families than it does for lower-income families because the higher-income earners generally have higher marginal tax rates, so a deduction against their taxable income leads to greater tax benefits.

Equivalent-to-Spouse Credit

The Equivalent-to-Spouse Credit[23] (formerly known as the Equivalent-to-Married Credit) is a non-refundable tax credit designed to reduce the financial burden on single parents who are raising children alone.[24] The credit is administered by Revenue Canada through the tax system. More than three million Canadians receive the Equivalent-to-Spouse Credit.[25] It is estimated that this credit cost the federal government $465 million in foregone revenues, and the provinces about another $270 million during the 1996 tax year.[26]

Recipients of the Equivalent-to-Spouse Credit must be single, divorced, separated, or widowed. As well, they must be responsible for a dependent child under the age of 18, or a dependant of any age with an infirmity, including aging parents or grandparents. They must also be a resident of Canada.

For the 1996 taxation year, the Equivalent-to-Spouse Credit was worth a maximum of $1,453 in federal and provincial tax savings, depending on the province.[27] However, not everyone is eligible for the maximum credit. The maximum is reduced when a dependent child under the age of 18 has an annual income in excess of $538. The credit becomes progressively smaller and disappears entirely when the dependant's income surpasses $5,918. The maximum is also reduced for claimants who have a dependant with an infirmity with *any* income, and it disappears once the dependant's income reaches $6,456.

Provincial Benefits for Families with Children

The provinces and territories provide roughly $2 billion in benefits for families with children through their own social assistance programs (see Chapter 2). As well, *most* provinces provide additional benefits through income and earnings supplements for low-income families, and through in-kind benefits such as supplemental health, dental, and prescription drug coverage, and child care assistance. Several provinces have announced new programs or major changes in their programs for families with children for the near future, and some are scheduled to coincide with the introduction of the new Canada Child Tax Benefit.[28]

The following is a brief overview of the provincial child benefit programs and related supports that were in place in mid-1997, along with the announced changes that were to come into effect later in 1997 and 1998.[29]

Nova Scotia[30]
In its 1994 budget, the Nova Scotia government introduced the Low-Income Tax Reduction Program for all low-income

households in the province, including additional tax benefits for families with children. In its 1997 budget, the tax reduction amounts were increased.

The current maximum tax reduction is $300 a year for the first adult, plus $165 for a second adult or child, and another $165 for each additional child in the family. The maximum tax reduction is available to families with incomes of up to $15,000 who have children. Families that do not benefit from the tax reduction program because their incomes are too low to pay taxes are eligible for a separate annual benefit of $125 per family. This amount, administered through the Nova Scotia Direct Assistance Program, is paid to families with incomes below $16,500.

New Brunswick[31]
In its spring 1997 budget, the province of New Brunswick announced its own Child Tax Benefit and Working Income Supplement to complement the Canada Child Tax Benefit. The first payments were made in October 1997 to New Brunswick residents who received the federal child benefits.

The eligibility requirements for the New Brunswick Child Tax Benefit and Working Income Supplement are the same as those used for the current federal Child Tax Benefit and Working Income Supplement, respectively. Those who are registered for the federal CTB automatically receive the New Brunswick CTB. The benefits are administered by Revenue Canada.

Following an initial lump-sum payment made to all eligible families in October 1997 (for the period April to October 1997), payments will be made monthly. The maximum monthly New Brunswick CTB has been slated at $21 per family ($250 a year). This maximum is reduced for families with annual incomes above $20,000. The maximum monthly WIS is also $21 per family. As with the federal WIS, the New Brunswick WIS is tied to earnings and is paid only to families with incomes below $25,921.

Quebec[32]

In January 1997, the government of Quebec announced the most comprehensive family policy and child benefits system in the country. As part of its reform package, the province stated that it would make major new investments in early childhood education, child care, maternity leave, and income supports, including a new integrated family allowance.

The cornerstone of the income support component is the New Family Allowance. Starting in September 1997, the New Family Allowance replaces the portion of social assistance paid to families on behalf of children, in addition to replacing several different family/child allowances.[33]

As part of the reform package, eligible families in Quebec still receive benefits under the existing Parental Wage Assistance program (an earnings supplementation program for low-income families with children), but these benefits have been adjusted to mesh with the new integrated allowance. As well, all Quebec families with children continue to receive the Quebec Child Tax Credit.

The New Family Allowance is paid to all low-income families with children, regardless of their source(s) of income. In the case of two-parent families, the allowance pays up to $81 a month per child for a first and second child ($975 a year), and $33 a month per child for a third and subsequent children ($398 a year). Single-parent families are eligible for an additional lump sum of up to $108 a month ($1,300 a year). Maximum benefits are paid to two-parent families with incomes of $21,825 or less, and to single-parent families with incomes of $15,332 or less. Benefits decline when family income surpasses these levels, and they eventually disappear as family income approaches $60,000, depending on the number of children.[34]

The new allowance is paid monthly, and it is determined according to the recipient's previous year's tax return. To be eligible, Quebec families with children must therefore file their tax returns and apply to receive the new allowance. It is paid automatically in the following years. The New Family Allowance is not taxable.

Along with the New Family Allowance, all Quebec families continue to receive the Child Tax Credit when they file their taxes each year. The maximum Child Tax Credit is worth $520 for the first child and $480 for subsequent children. Single-parent families receive an extra $260.[35] The Child Tax Credit is not income tested. It is the only universal tax credit for families with children in Canada.

Eligible low-income families with children also continue to receive support through the Parental Wage Assistance Program. These families receive a supplement of 28.5 cents for each dollar in work earnings above $1,200. The maximum supplement is $3,534 for a couple with children, and $2,422 for a single parent with children. Couples with incomes of up to $13,600 and single-parent families with incomes up to $9,700 are eligible for the maximum supplement. The supplement is reduced by 43 cents for each dollar in earnings above the upper-income thresholds, until it disappears entirely at incomes of $21,825 for couples and $15,332 for single parents.

Ontario[36]
In its 1997 spring budget, the government of Ontario announced a new refundable Child Care Tax Credit, as well as an enhancement of the Ontario Tax Reduction program for low-income families with children.

For the 1997 tax year, the Child Care Tax Credit will cover 25 per cent of qualifying child-care expenses for children under the age of seven, up to a maximum credit of $400. (Criteria for eligible expenses match those used for the federal Child Care Expense Deduction.) The maximum is paid to families with incomes of up to $20,000. The province of Ontario has stated that the new credit will be enriched as the federal government increases funding for the new Canada Child Tax Benefit.

13

Ontario also offers a reduction in taxes for low-income families with children. The 1997 provincial budget lowered the amount of the tax reduction per family, but expanded the number of low-income families eligible for tax relief. For the 1997 tax year, the basic tax reduction will be $171, plus an additional $334 for each dependent child under the age of 18 or each dependant with a disability. The basic reduction for the 1998 tax year will be $161, plus an additional $331 for each eligible dependant.

Manitoba[37]
Since 1981, the province of Manitoba has had an income supplementation program in place for low-income families with dependent children.[38] The Child Related Income Support Program (CRISP) provides a supplement to families that are eligible for the federal Child Tax Benefit. CRISP benefits are paid monthly, and recipients must reapply each year.

The 1997 maximum CRISP benefit was $30 per month for each child under the age of 18 (or $360 a year). Families with one child and an income below $14,188 were eligible for the maximum benefit. With each additional child, the family income limit for maximum benefit eligibility rises by approximately $1,000. CRISP benefits are phased out as family income rises above these thresholds, depending on the number of children in the family.

Families are also eligible for a tax reduction of $250 for each child under the age of 18 when they file their returns each year. Higher-income families with children can reduce their surtaxes by claiming an additional $25 per child. There is also a Manitoba Cost of Living Credit worth $25 per child per year.

Saskatchewan[39]
In the spring of 1997, the province of Saskatchewan announced that it would introduce its own child benefit and employment supplement to top-up the Canada Child Tax Benefit proposed by the federal government. As well, the province stated that it would extend in-kind supports such as dental and health

benefits to all low-income families, regardless of their source(s) of income.

The Saskatchewan Child Benefit is to be introduced in 1998 to coincide with the implementation of the Canada Child Tax Benefit. It will be a monthly benefit, paid on a per-child basis to all low-income families in the province. When the Saskatchewan Child Benefit is introduced, it will replace both the current Saskatchewan Family Income Plan – its current child benefit program – and the portion of social assistance paid on behalf of children.

As part of the transition to the new integrated system of provincial and federal child benefits, Saskatchewan Family Income Plan benefits were increased in May 1997 from $105 to $120 per month per child, or from $1,260 to $1,440 a year. Children's health benefits under the Saskatchewan Family Income Plan were also extended to provide full health coverage for these families.

In addition to the Saskatchewan Child Benefit, the provincial government has said it will introduce the Saskatchewan Employment Supplement in 1998 for families with work earnings. Like the Saskatchewan Child Benefit, the Saskatchewan Employment Supplement will be a monthly benefit that will vary with the number of children in each family. It will also vary according to family earnings, including child support income.

The province also provides the Saskatchewan Child Tax Reduction for low- and modest-income families with children. Families with incomes below $40,000 are eligible for a tax reduction of $250 per child, up to a maximum of $1,000 when they file their tax returns each year.

Alberta[40]
In January 1997, the Alberta government unveiled a new earned income supplement for all low-wage families with children in

the province – the Alberta Family Employment Tax Credit. Under this program, eligible families receive an advance payment each July and January for the coming six months. The first payments were made in July 1997, retroactive to January 1997.

The Alberta Family Tax Credit is paid automatically to families with children who are eligible for the federal Child Tax Benefit, and who meet established earnings and income requirements. The credit is paid to families with earnings of at least $6,500, based on the previous tax year. In 1997, the maximum credit was paid to families with incomes between $13,000 and $25,000, after which it gradually decreased to zero for those with incomes above $37,500. The upper-income threshold will rise to $50,000 in 1998. Those eligible for the maximum credit in 1997 received a single payment in July of $250 per child, up to a maximum of $500 per family. Starting in 1998, the payments will be made on a semi-annual basis, and the maximum amounts will be doubled.

British Columbia[41]

In November 1995, the province of British Columbia announced a major overhaul of its social assistance system. An important component of this reform package was the introduction of an income supplement for low- and modest-income families with children – the Family Bonus. Along with the income support package, the BC government also introduced a new Healthy Kids program designed to provide health, dental, and vision care for all children in low-income families.

The British Columbia Family Bonus is paid as part of the federal Child Tax Benefit cheque to all low-income families in the province, regardless of their source(s) of income. The Family Bonus replaced the children's portion of provincial social assistance payments, while extending new benefits for low-income families that rely primarily on employment earnings. The 1997 maximum benefit of $103 a month ($1,236 per year) was paid to one- and two-child families with incomes of $18,000 per year or less. The bonus was phased out thereafter until it disappeared when family income reached $32,000. (The income thresholds were higher for families with more than two children.)

Endnotes

1. Unless otherwise stated, information for this section was taken from: Ken Battle and Leon Muszynski, *One Way to Fight Child Poverty* (Ottawa: Caledon Institute of Social Policy, 1995, pp. 8-9); Dennis Guest, *The Emergence of Social Security in Canada* (Vancouver: University of British Columbia Press, 1985); and, David Ross, *The Working Poor: Wage Earners and the Failure of Income Security Policies* (Ottawa: The Canadian Institute for Economic Policy Studies, 1981).

2. *Inventory of Income Security Programs in Canada* (Ottawa: Human Resources Development Canada, January 1993).

3. Unless otherwise stated, information in this section was taken from *Budget 1997 – Working Together Towards a National Child Benefits System* (Ottawa: Government of Canada, 1997); *Budget Plan* (Ottawa: Government of Canada, 1997); *Your Child Tax Benefit* (Ottawa: Revenue Canada, 1996); and, *Information Sheet for the Child Tax Benefit Application* (Ottawa: Government of Canada, 1996).

4. *Budget Plan* (Ottawa: Government of Canada, 1997, p. 107).

5. In addition to being a resident of Canada, either the applicant or their spouse must be a Canadian citizen, landed immigrant, convention refugee, a visitor to Canada, or have a Minister's permit and have lived in Canada for at least 1 1/2 years.

6. In order to be eligible for the Child Tax Benefit, applicants must file a tax return.

7. "Income" refers to the net income used for tax purposes: earnings, interest, and other income, less any deductions such as RRSPs and child care expenses. Although not treated as taxable income, workers' compensation benefits and social assistance income are also included in the net income amount. This definition applies to the use of the term income throughout this chapter.

8.   The age limit is higher for children with disabilities. As well, the $213 a year is reduced by 25 per cent of any amount claimed under the Child Care Expense Deduction.

9.   The maximum annual federal Child Tax Benefit in Alberta in 1997 was as follows: $935 for children under age seven; $1,004 for children between seven and 11; $1,333 for children aged 12 to 15; and, $1,205 for children aged 16 and 17. In Quebec, the maximum annual federal Child Tax Benefit was $869 for the first child, $1,000 for the second child, and $1,672 for the third and subsequent children. Although eligible families with one child in Quebec received lower federal benefits, other supports provided by the Quebec government more than offset the difference. The figures for Alberta come from a pamphlet entitled, *Alberta Family Employment Tax Credit* (Edmonton: Government of Alberta, 1997). The figures for Quebec are taken from *Families First - New Elements of the Family Policy* (Quebec City: Quebec Family Secretariat, 1997).

10.   "Earned income" for the purposes of calculating the Working Income Supplement includes the following: employment income, including tips and gratuities; net self-employment income; training allowances; the taxable portion of scholarships, bursaries, and similar awards; net research grants; any earnings supplement received under a project sponsored by the Government of Canada; and, disability benefits received from the Canada or Quebec Pension Plans.

11.   In 1997, the Working Income Supplement rose by 9.7 cents for each dollar in *annual family earnings* between $3,750 and $10,000 for a family with one child. It rose by 16.2 cents for a family with two children, and by 21.4 cents for a family with three or more children.

12.   In 1997, the Working Income Supplement was reduced by 12.1 cents for each dollar in *annual family income* above $20,921 for a family with one child; by 20.2 cents for a family with two children; and by 26.8 cents for a family with three or more children.

13.   Prior to July 1997, the Working Income Supplement was paid on a per family basis to a maximum of $500 per year per family. The 1997 February federal budget changed the WIS to a per child basis to pave the way for its proposed merger with the Child Tax Benefit to form the new Canada Child Tax Benefit.

14.   Unless otherwise stated, information for this section was taken from: *The National Child Benefit: Building a Better Future for Canadian Children* (Joint release of the Federal, Provincial and Territorial governments [excluding Quebec], September 1997); *Budget 1997 – Working Together Towards a National Child Benefits System* (Ottawa: Government of Canada, 1997); and, *Budget Plan* (Ottawa: Government of Canada, 1997).

15. *Budget Plan* (Ottawa: Government of Canada, 1997, p. 107). This includes the 1996 total of $5.1 billion spent on the combined Child Tax Benefit and Working Income Supplement, plus the $250 million increase in the WIS in July 1997 and the additional $650 million earmarked to boost the combined CTB/WIS benefit in July 1998.

16. This would include income from wages, social assistance, Employment Insurance, Workers' Compensation, Canada Pension Plan Disability, and so on.

17. *The National Child Benefit: Building a Better Future for Canadian Children* (Joint release of the Federal, Provincial and Territorial governments [excluding Quebec], September 1997).

18. Unless otherwise stated, information for this section was taken from *Child Care Expenses Information Sheet for 1996 - T1065E* (Ottawa: Revenue Canada, 1996).

19. The province of Quebec offers its own Child Care Expense Deduction. The Quebec deduction is being phased out as the province gradually implements wider access to low-cost child care.

20. *Taxation Statistics on Individuals - Tax Year 1995* (Ottawa: Revenue Canada, 1997).

21. *Personal and Corporate Tax Expenditures* (Ottawa: Department of Finance Canada, 1997). The provincial cost is estimated based on the average provincial tax rate of 58 per cent of the federal rate in 1996.

22. The definition of "earned income" for the Child Care Expense Deduction is the same as that used for the Child Tax Benefit. It includes: employment income including tips and gratuities; net self-employment income; training allowances; the taxable portion of scholarships, bursaries, and similar awards; net research grants; any earnings supplement received under a project sponsored by the Government of Canada; and, disability benefits received from the Canada or Quebec Pension Plans. See "Calculation of Child Care Expense Deduction," Form T778 E (Ottawa: Revenue Canada, 1997).

23. Unless otherwise stated, information for this section was taken from *The General Income Tax Guide – 96* (Ottawa: Government of Canada, 1997, p. 26).

24. The province of Quebec offers its own credit for single parents.

25. *Taxation Statistics on Individuals - Tax Year 1995* (Ottawa: Revenue Canada, 1997).

26. *Personal and Corporate Tax Expenditures* (Ottawa: Department of Finance Canada, 1997). The provincial cost is an estimate based on the 1996 average provincial tax rate of 58 per cent of the federal rate.

27. To calculate the maximum federal-provincial tax savings from the Equivalent-to-Spouse Credit, the Equivalent-to-Spouse amount was multiplied by the federal tax rate, plus provincial credit savings. The Equivalent-to-Spouse amount was $5,380 for the 1996 tax year. The average provincial tax rate in 1996 was 58 per cent of the federal rate, making the average joint federal-provincial tax credit rate approximately 27 per cent. Hence, the maximum credit of $1,453 ($5,380 x .27). Note that the 1997 average provincial tax rate was 54 per cent of the federal rate.

28. *Budget 1997 - Working Together Towards a National Child Benefit System* (Ottawa: Government of Canada, 1997, p. 13).

29. The following section outlines provincial supplements that apply generally to all low-income families with children. Several jurisdictions have in place child benefits that are designed specifically for families with dependent children that have disabilities. These specific disability-related programs are not covered in this section.

30. Unless otherwise stated, information for this section was taken from the *Nova Scotia Budget 97 Bulletin* (Halifax: Government of Nova Scotia, 1997), and supplemented by discussions with officials in the Nova Scotia Department of Finance. For further information regarding the Direct Assistance Program, contact Nova Scotia Business and Consumer Services.

31. Unless otherwise stated, information for this section was taken from *1997-1998 Budget, Province of New Brunswick* (Fredericton: Government of New Brunswick, April 1997).

32. Unless otherwise stated, information for this section was taken from: *Families First - New Elements of the Family Policy* (Quebec: Quebec Family Secretariat, 1997); *The Income Security Reform: The Road to Labour Market Entry, Training and Employment* (Quebec: Government of Quebec, 1996); and, *The New Family Allowance and Income Security* (Quebec: Ministère de l'Emploi et de la Solidarité, 1997). These sources were supplemented by interviews with officials from the Quebec Ministry of Income Security.

33. Quebec's New Family Allowance replaces the existing Quebec Family Allowance, the Allowance for Young Children, and Allowances for Newborn Children.

34. The reduction rate for Quebec's New Family Allowance is not based on a gradual, steady decline. For example, for a first and second child, the reduction rate is calculated as follows: 50 per cent for income between the threshold ($21,825 for

couples and $15,332 for single-parent families) and $20,921; 30 per cent for income between $20,921 and $25,921; and 50 per cent for income above $25,921 until benefits disappear.

35. Note that the value of the universal child credits in Quebec are calculated as 20 per cent of what the provincial government refers to as "essential needs." These essential needs are identified as the following: $2,600 for the first child in a two-parent family; $2,400 for subsequent children; and an extra flat amount of $1,300 for single parents.

36. Unless otherwise stated, information for this section was taken from *1997 Ontario Budget* and *1997 Ontario Budget: Budget Speech* (Toronto: Government of Ontario, May 1997).

37. Unless otherwise stated, information for this section was taken from: *Child Related Income Support Program* (brochure); *Child Related Income Support Program: Application Guidelines, July 1997-June 1988* (Winnipeg: Manitoba Family Services, 1997); and, the 1996 Manitoba Income Tax form.

38. *Inventory of Income Security Programs in Canada* (Ottawa: Human Resources Development Canada, 1993).

39. Unless otherwise stated, information for this section was taken from *Children, Families and Independence – Social Assistance Redesign* (Regina: Government of Saskatchewan, March 1997), and from the 1996 Saskatchewan Income Tax form.

40. Unless otherwise stated, information for this section was taken from a pamphlet entitled, *Alberta Family Employment Tax Credit* (Edmonton: Government of Alberta, 1997). The information was supplemented by an interview with an official from the Alberta branch of Revenue Canada.

41. Unless otherwise stated, the information for this section was taken from *The British Columbia Family Bonus – Backgrounder Information for the 1996 Annual Premier's Conference* (Victoria: Province of British Columbia, August 1996), and from *British Columbia's Proposal for a National Child Benefit* (Victoria: Province of British Columbia, February 1997).

Chapter 2
Social Assistance and Other Income Supports

Background

In the early part of the century, local private charities and emergency public "relief" offered by local government officials were the only types of assistance available to individuals in Canada who found themselves without any means of support.[1] The assistance was usually temporary and offered "in-kind" support, including such items as food and second-hand clothing. Direct cash assistance and more permanent forms of aid were rare. This informal system reflected the prevailing view that poverty was generally the result of improper budgeting and other personal inadequacies, and that long-term help would generate dependence.[2]

The two World Wars and the Great Depression changed Canadians' views about the causes of poverty and the means to address it. The social and economic disruptions of this period led many people to conclude that perhaps poverty had less to do with individual inadequacies and more to do with the uncertainties inherent in daily life. Increasingly, Canadians turned to governments to reduce this uncertainty and help provide for those who, for whatever reason, were unable to provide for themselves.

Between the 1920s and the 1940s, a number of new programs designed to support Canada's most vulnerable citizens came into existence. Following the First World War, the federal government introduced financial supports for disabled soldiers and their families, and for the widows and children of soldiers who had died overseas. In the 1920s, several provincial governments instituted Mothers' Pensions for single mothers. After the Second World War, the federal government introduced veterans' allowances and assistance for persons with disabilities. For the able-bodied unemployed worker who fell outside of these categories and was not eligible for Unemployment Insurance (which was inaugurated in 1941), an unemployment assistance program was established jointly by the federal and provincial governments in 1956.

By the 1960s, it was recognized that Canada had developed a confusing and inadequate maze of federal, provincial, and local supports for people in need. In an attempt to consolidate this range of support programs for specific groups – including the elderly, the long-term unemployed, persons with disabilities, and single mothers – and extend assistance to those who fell outside of these established categories, the federal government introduced a new cost-sharing arrangement with the provinces in 1966 – the Canada Assistance Plan (CAP). The Canada Assistance Plan brought together all of the federal-provincial cost-shared programs that had been offered on a means, or needs-tested, basis into one comprehensive program of supports. It was referred to as "welfare" or "social assistance" and was designed to meet the financial needs of the recipients, regardless of their reasons for seeking help.

The Canada Assistance Plan established three national standards to guide spending on provincial programs, as well as a set of administrative requirements. The three national standards were the following:

- Assistance must be provided to anyone "in need" (determined by needs test).

- Applicants could not be denied assistance because they came from outside of the province where they were seeking assistance (now referred to as "guaranteed mobility rights").
- Applicants had to have the opportunity to appeal decisions regarding their application for assistance.

The federal government agreed to match half of all the provincial expenditures on programs that met these national standards, without limits.

Full federal-provincial cost-sharing of social assistance under the Canada Assistance Plan prevailed until severe strains on the system began to be felt in the 1980s. The cost to the federal government of this open-ended commitment to share expenses had risen substantially, as provincial social assistance caseloads expanded with rising unemployment, and program costs grew as benefits were enriched. The social assistance caseload rose from about six per cent of the population in the early 1980s, to over 10 per cent by the early 1990s.[3] The cost of social assistance more than doubled during this period.[4]

To control these costs, the federal government introduced a "cap on CAP" between 1990 and 1995. With this cap, the federal government limited its social assistance contributions to an increase of five per cent a year for the country's three wealthiest provinces – Ontario, Alberta, and British Columbia. As a result, the federal contribution to social assistance in those provinces quickly fell well below the previous level of 50 per cent. By the mid-1990s, this had created substantial inequities in the funds transferred by the federal government to the so-called "have" and "have-not" provinces.

In 1996, the federal government created the Canada Health and Social Transfer (CHST) by combining the Canada Assistance Plan with the Established Programs Financing (EPF) – the federal transfer for health and post-secondary education. The CHST eliminated all but one of the national standards for social assistance that had been contained in the Canada Assistance

Plan – guaranteed mobility rights. Rather than CAP's cost-sharing provision, a block funding arrangement was adopted similar to that of the EPF. At the same time, the cash portion of the transfer was reduced substantially.

Current Social Assistance Programs

Social assistance, or welfare as it is commonly known, is often referred to as a program of "last resort."[5] It is a form of modest financial assistance provided to individuals and families who would otherwise be unable to sustain themselves. In general, Canadians turn to social assistance once they have exhausted all other public and private means of support. In 1996, nearly 10 per cent of the Canadian population was in receipt of social assistance benefits.[6] The cost of providing these benefits totalled $13.7 billion for the 1995-96 fiscal year.[7]

Jurisdictional Responsibilities

Social assistance is primarily a provincial and territorial concern in Canada. The federal government's main role is to provide financial contributions to the provinces and territories via the Canada Health and Social Transfer (CHST) and Territorial Formula Financing.[8] The federal government also provides funding to Aboriginal Band Councils (and in some cases, to provincial governments) who, in turn, provide social assistance to Aboriginal people on reserves. These programs generally mirror the provincial and territorial programs in which the Bands are located.[9] Since each province and territory is responsible for its own social assistance system, there are substantial variations in the rules and regulations governing social assistance benefits across the country. Currently, the only national standard that guides federal transfers to the provinces and territories for social assistance is the guarantee of mobility rights of all Canadians.[10]

Although all provinces and territories are responsible for administering social assistance, some have delegated a portion of this responsibility to their local levels of government. In Nova Scotia, Manitoba, and Ontario, for example, local governments administer short-term and emergency assistance to employable recipients, while the provincial governments offer long-term assistance to individuals who are deemed unemployable, such as single parents with young children, the elderly, and persons with disabilities. This joint local-provincial administrative structure is often referred to as a "two-tiered" system.

The two-tiered model now appears to be disappearing in Canada. In the spring of 1997, the Nova Scotia government began taking full administrative control over social assistance. At the same time, the Ontario government announced its intention to do exactly the opposite. The Ontario government said that it would hand over full administrative responsibility for social assistance programming to local governments, while continuing to set the broad rules for the system and cover 80 per cent of the costs.[11] In the fall of 1997, the Manitoba government introduced legislation that would give it full administrative control over social assistance in that province.

Eligibility

When applying for social assistance benefits, individuals are required to submit financial and personal information to the agency or department responsible for administering the benefits in their area. This information generally includes proof of age, medical confirmation of a disability, and cheque stubs or bank account information as proof of income, depending on the circumstances. Once an application has been reviewed, a caseworker or agency representative assigns the applicant to a particular client category and determines their eligibility for support.

In order to qualify for social assistance benefits, applicants must meet a "needs test" which takes into consideration both their household assets and income. In each jurisdiction, the value of a claimant's household assets must not exceed established limits, and their financial resources must be deemed inadequate to cover their basic personal needs such as food, clothing, and shelter. Among other items, an applicant's primary residence and car (within certain limits) are generally exempt from the overall needs test. Increasingly over the last several years, these "asset exemptions" have been restricted in certain jurisdictions, including British Columbia, Alberta, and Ontario.[12] The exemptions for liquid assets such as investments or savings in a bank account have been scaled back the most.

Social assistance applicants are commonly divided into four categories: the elderly, persons with disabilities, single-parent families, and unemployed employable persons. The category to which an applicant is assigned largely determines what they must do in order to begin, and continue, receiving benefits.

As a precondition for receiving benefits, employable applicants are usually required to enter into a contract of mutual responsibility with their local social assistance department or agency. In this contract, the responsibilities of the potential recipient and those of the social assistance provider are outlined. As part of this agreement, the recipient is often expected to undertake one or more activities such as skills upgrading, counselling, or a job search. Recently, this list has been expanded in a number of jurisdictions to include job placement and community service activities. Quebec, British Columbia, Alberta, New Brunswick, and Ontario are provinces that have moved in this direction.

Employable applicants who seek social assistance because they have quit or been dismissed from their job usually have to wait for their benefits, and in some cases, they are denied assistance entirely.[13] In Ontario and the Northwest Territories, for example, a three-month waiting period is now required before employable applicants can collect social assistance benefits. Alberta simply denies benefits to individuals in similar circumstances, and officials in Saskatchewan have the authority to deny benefits to employable applicants who leave their job for "insufficient reasons."

Over the last few years, the lines that traditionally have separated the categories of employable and unemployable have shifted. For example, a number of jurisdictions have reclassified large numbers of single parents who receive social assistance from unemployable to employable. Once they are grouped with other employable recipients, these single parents are expected to meet the standard requirements of the employable category such as engaging in job search and training activities. Now, single parents with young children – generally school-aged or older – are classified as employable in most jurisdictions in Canada, including British Columbia, Quebec, Manitoba, the Yukon, Ontario, and Alberta.

Traditionally, persons with disabilities were also considered to be unemployable, but some are now being reclassified as employable in Quebec, British Columbia, and Ontario. In these jurisdictions, officials are tightening the definition of "disability," and in the process, they are dropping individuals with less severe disabilities from the unemployable caseload. Some provinces, including Ontario, Alberta, and British Columbia, are establishing separate income support plans that are outside of the welfare system – and pay higher benefits – for persons with severe disabilities.

The elderly – generally defined as persons aged 60 and older – continue to be classified as unemployable, just as they have in the past. Other than the basic age requirement and a means test, there were few other requirements that the elderly had to meet in order to receive social assistance benefits. Recently, however, all jurisdictions have introduced a requirement that seniors over the age of 60 must apply for Canada or Quebec Pension Plan retirement benefits before they can be considered for social assistance support. (CPP/QPP benefits are provided at a reduced rate for seniors between the ages of 60 and 65.)

Young people under 18 years who receive social assistance benefits, not including those with disabilities, have been expected to meet similar requirements to those of employable adults, such as participating in work-search and training programs. As well, if they were still in school, certain standards for attendance and performance were applied. This has not changed in recent years, but there is a new requirement in several jurisdictions that applicants under the age of 18 must be enrolled in school *and* under adult supervision before they are considered eligible for social assistance. As well, most jurisdictions are now intensifying efforts to ensure that young people are in either training or work placements. Some areas, such as British Columbia and Saskatchewan, have even introduced new income and training support programs to replace social assistance for youth.

Overall, eligibility for social assistance has become more stringent in recent years. In most jurisdictions, applicants are subjected to tighter controls and more intensive and intrusive scrutiny by government officials than in the past. Increasingly in the 1990s, jurisdictions are relying on more frequent – and in some cases, unannounced – home visits by caseworkers, new fraud or "welfare snitch" hotlines, mandatory cheque pick-ups, extensive case reviews, and new powers for agents verifying claims as efforts to reduce what some people view as widespread abuse of the welfare system. How effective these efforts have been in providing greater efficiency and less abuse in the welfare system is the subject of ongoing debate (as is debate about the degree to which fraud and abuse exist in the system).

Benefits

Social assistance benefits come primarily in two forms: basic assistance and special assistance. Basic or regular assistance generally includes monthly amounts for food, clothing, shelter, utilities, and personal and household needs. (Some jurisdictions separate the amounts allocated for shelter from those of other basic needs when calculating total assistance.) In addition to basic assistance, some categories of recipients are eligible for supplemental benefits, commonly referred to as "special assistance." These supports generally include extra monthly income assistance for persons with disabilities, and seasonal supports such as money for school expenses, winter clothing allowances, and Christmas allowances. Neither basic nor special assistance is treated as taxable income (except for certain categories of recipients in Quebec, beginning in 1998).

Social assistance benefits are reduced if recipients have income from employment earnings above a threshold amount, referred to as the "earnings exemption." Earnings exemptions – and thus the amount of money that can be earned without affecting one's social assistance benefits – have been increased in some parts of the country in recent years in order to encourage employable recipients to take on part-time and temporary work.

The amount of income support provided to eligible social assistance applicants varies according to a number of factors, including family size, the age of children, and the employability of the recipient. Table 1 provides estimates of provincial and territorial basic and special assistance for four categories of social assistance recipients in 1997: a single employable person; a person with a disability; a single parent with one child; and, a couple with two children. Because these estimates are based on maximum amounts, specific individuals in the sample categories would not necessarily be eligible for the benefit levels indicated here. This comparison is based on methodology used by the National Council of Welfare in its annual publication, *Welfare Incomes*.[14]

This comparison includes only provincial and territorial *income* benefits paid *automatically* to the various categories of eligible social assistance applicants. It does not include in-kind supports such as dental and medical assistance, or one-time emergency supports or discretionary payments such as those for funeral or moving costs. Monthly cash benefits (not including tax credits or tax reductions) paid through provincial child benefit programs on behalf of children in low-income families *are* included in the comparison. In 1997, such benefits were available in British Columbia, Quebec, and New Brunswick (see Chapter 1).[15] The federal Child Tax Benefit, which is available in all provinces and territories, is *not* included in this comparison.

Table 1

Estimated Annual Provincial/Territorial Social Assistance Income Benefits, by Type of Household, 1997			
Province/Territory	Basic Social Assistance ($)	Special Assistance ($)	Total Social Assistance: Basic + Special Assistance ($)
Newfoundland Single Employable Person with a Disability Single Parent, One Child Couple, Two Children	4,326 6,810 11,262 12,186	1,500[1]	4,326 8,310 11,262 12,186
Prince Edward Island Single Employable Person with a Disability Single Parent, One Child Couple, Two Children	5,316 7,836[2] 9,972 14,976	1,092[3]	5,316 8,928 9,972 14,976
Nova Scotia Single Employable Person with a Disability Single Parent, One Child Couple, Two Children	4,428 8,568 9,372 13,992		4,428 8,568 9,372 13,992
New Brunswick Single Employable Person with a Disability Single Parent, One Child Couple, Two Children	3,168[4] 6,663[4] 8,772 9,828	1,200[5] 1,500[6]	3,168 6,663 9,972 11,328
Quebec Single Employable Person with a Disability Single Parent, One Child Couple, Two Children	5,910 8,388 10,188[7] 11,954[8]	738[9] 877[10]	5,910 8,388 10,926 12,831
Ontario Single Employable Person with a Disability Single Parent, One Child Couple, Two Children	6,240 11,160 11,484 14,568	105[11] 407[12]	6,240 11,160 11,589 14,975
See Notes for Table 1 on page 35			

Province/Territory	Basic Social Assistance ($)	Special Assistance ($)	Total Social Assistance: Basic + Special Assistance ($)
Manitoba			
Single Employable	5,352		5,352
Person with a Disability	6,478	1,519	7,997
Single Parent, One Child	8,777	859	9,636
Couple, Two Children	14,232 [13]		14,232
Saskatchewan			
Single Employable	5,760		5,760
Person with a Disability	7,500		7,500
Single Parent, One Child	10,381	50 [14]	10,431
Couple, Two Children	14,643	215 [15]	14,858
Alberta			
Single Employable	4,764		4,764
Person with a Disability	9,768 [16]		9,768
Single Parent, One Child	9,324		9,324
Couple, Two Children	14,592	150 [17]	14,742
British Columbia			
Single Employable	6,046	35 [18]	6,081
Person with a Disability	9,252	35 [18]	9,287
Single Parent, One Child	10,548	1,316 [19]	11,864
Couple, Two Children	12,996	2,662 [20]	15,658
Yukon			
Single Employable	7,740	155 [21]	7,895
Person with a Disability	7,740	1,655 [22]	9,395
Single Parent, One Child	12,540	572 [23]	13,112
Couple, Two Children	19,080	685 [24]	19,765
Northwest Territories			
Single Employable	7,740		7,740
Person with a Disability	7,740	1,800	9,540
Single Parent, One Child	17,316		17,316
Couple, Two Children	21,660		21,660

Source: Various provincial and territorial ministries responsible for social assistance, and the Social Program Information and Analysis Division, Strategic Policy Branch of Human Resources Development Canada.

See Notes for Table 1 on page 35

Notes for Table 1

1. This is a flat-rate monthly supplement of $125 for a single person with a disability who requires supportive services to aid independent living.
2. This includes a special housing allowance for persons with disabilities who have special housing needs. Contact the PEI Department of Health and Social Services for more information.
3. Includes $51 a month for personal expenses and $40 a month special allowance paid to persons with disabilities. Up to an additional $150 a month is available for families that must care for a child with an infirmity. For more information, contact the PEI Department of Health and Social Services.
4. Incorporates the rate changes effective April 1997, for single individuals and two-adult families with no children.
5. Includes a $900 supplement for families with children, plus $250 for the New Brunswick Child Tax Benefit (broken into monthly instalments), plus a $50 school supplies supplement.
6. Includes a $900 supplement for families with children, plus $250 per child for the New Brunswick Child Tax Benefit, plus a $50 school supplies supplement for each child.
7. Includes Quebec's Income Security Benefit ($9,105), plus an adjustment paid to families with children in receipt of income security benefits ($324), in addition to the New Family Allowance paid to all low-income families with children ($81.25 a month per child, plus a $108.33 a month supplement for single parents, both beginning in September 1997).
8. Includes Quebec's Income Security Benefit ($10,910), plus an adjustment for families with children in receipt of income security benefits ($394), plus the New Family Allowance ($81.25 per child, starting in September).
9. Includes allowance for housing ($60 a month from January to September 1997, then $66 a month for the remainder of the year).
10. Includes the housing allowance plus a school allowance ($46 for the younger child and $93 for the older child).
11. Winter clothing allowance.
12. Includes a winter clothing allowance ($105 per child) and a back-to-school allowance ($69 for the younger child and $128 for the older child).
13. The City of Winnipeg eliminated its top-up to the children's rates (except for infants) effective May 15, 1997. The top-up is therefore included for 4.5 months.
14. School supply amount.
15. School supply amount for younger child is $85, plus $130 for the older child.
16. Persons with severe disabilities receive support through a separate program called the Assured Income for the Severely Handicapped (AISH) which pays benefits that are higher than those in the regular income support program. The AISH benefit level is used for these calculations. Note that the annual estimate takes into consideration the July 1997 increase in the monthly AISH benefit (from $810 to $818).
17. School supply amount.
18. Christmas allowance.
19. Includes a BC Family Bonus amount of $1,236 ($103 per child per month), plus an $80 Christmas allowance ($70 for a family with dependent children, plus $10 per child).
20. Includes a BC Family Bonus amount of $2,472, plus $90 Christmas allowance, and $100 for school supplies ($42 for younger child, $58 for older child).
21. Includes Christmas allowance of $30 and winter clothing allowance of $125.
22. Includes Christmas allowance of $30, winter clothing allowance of $125, and a supplementary allowance of $125 a month for persons with disabilities who are permanently excluded from the labour market.
23. Includes Christmas allowance of $30 per person, winter clothing allowance of $75 for the child and $125 for the adult, and $312 for babysitting throughout the year.
24. Includes Christmas allowance of $30 per person, winter clothing allowance of $75 for younger child and $125 for the older child and the two adults, as well as school supply allowances of $50 and $65.

In general, social assistance benefit levels have remained the same or decreased over the last few years. Ontario and Alberta are often used as examples of the trend towards lower assistance levels but they are not the only jurisdictions that have scaled back support. Since the early 1990s, single employable persons have seen their benefits cut in all provinces and territories. Persons with disabilities have been spared, for the most part, from direct benefit cuts, as have persons in other "unemployable" categories such as recipients with young children and the elderly.

In addition to reductions in basic social assistance rates, many jurisdictions have also cut back on special assistance, in-kind supports such as dental and prescription drug assistance, and various emergency supports in recent years. However, a number of jurisdictions are now showing a renewed interest in providing other in-kind supports, especially for children. These supports are unlikely to be delivered through the welfare system, as provinces such as Quebec, British Columbia, and Saskatchewan experiment with new forms of in-kind supports and services for *all* low-income families with children. These new initiatives are at the heart of discussions concerning a new National Child Benefit System (see Chapter 1).

As shown earlier in Table 1, social assistance benefits (basic and special) tend to be highest in the Yukon and the Northwest Territories where the cost of living is very high. By contrast, benefit levels in the Atlantic provinces tend to be at the low end of the scale. While unemployment in the Atlantic is generally high, and thus the demand for benefits is also high, the cost of living tends to be lower in this region than in other parts of the country. Nevertheless, the lower cost of living in the Atlantic provinces does not account for the full, and often substantial, variations in the rates paid.

The annual social assistance rates for single employable persons range from a low of $3,168 in New Brunswick to a high of $7,895 in the Yukon. Even after the cuts to social assistance in

Ontario in 1995, the benefit levels in that province remain among the highest in the country, but far behind those in the Yukon and Northwest Territories, where the cost of living is significantly higher than elsewhere in the country. Conversely, following social assistance cuts in Alberta in the early 1990s, benefit levels for single employable persons in that province are among the lowest in Canada.

In 1997, the assistance rates for persons with disabilities ranged from a low of $6,663 in New Brunswick to a high of $11,160 in Ontario. That same year, Ontario introduced – but had not yet implemented – legislation to remove persons with severe disabilities from the social assistance caseloads. Alberta, on the other hand, had already implemented a separate plan for persons with severe disabilities – the Assured Income for Severely Handicapped Program (AISH) – and the benefit levels reflect that change. As shown in Table 1, the benefit paid under AISH to a single person with a disability ($9,768) places Alberta near the top of the rate scale, second only to Ontario.

In 1997, a single parent with one child was eligible for assistance ranging from a low of $9,324 in Alberta to a high of $17,316 in the Northwest Territories, followed by the Yukon ($13,112) and British Columbia ($11,864). As was noted in Chapter 1, the federal Child Tax Benefit was lower in Quebec than elsewhere in the country, which affects comparisons between Quebec and other provinces in the "single parent" and the "couple, two children" categories. In Alberta as well, the federal Child Tax Benefit varied according to the age of the children.

When considering social assistance benefits paid to a couple with two children, the Northwest Territories and the Yukon stand out with the highest rates by far – paying $21,660 and $19,765 a year, respectively. British Columbia's combination of social assistance, plus the BC Family Bonus, makes it the highest rate for this category among the provinces (paying families a total of $15,658), but it is still lower than the rate in

37

the two territories. Ontario, Alberta, Saskatchewan, and Prince Edward Island followed closely behind British Columbia, with each providing close to $15,000 a year to eligible families in this category.

Although Quebec offers relatively low benefit levels to families with children under its combination of social assistance and the New Family Allowance, the province does have the most generous package of tax supports for low-income families with children in the country (see Chapter 1). Families with children receive the lowest benefits in New Brunswick ($11,328), even after the province's new Child Tax Benefit is included.

Other Income Supports

In addition to social assistance, which forms the basis of Canada's social safety net, other forms of financial assistance are available to particular categories of persons. Two major areas of support are benefits designed to assist persons with disabilities and benefits for war veterans. This section also highlights the Goods and Services Tax Credit which was established to offset the impact of the Goods and Services Tax (GST) on individuals and families with low incomes.

Supports for Persons with Disabilities

As outlined in other sections in this book, a number of income security programs offer financial and other forms of support to persons with disabilities, including provincial social assistance programs (Chapter 2) and Workers' Compensation plans (Chapter 3), the Canada Pension Plan (Chapter 4), and the Veteran's Disability Pension program (Chapter 2). In addition to the income and service supports received under these programs, persons with disabilities also benefit from a range of measures in the tax system.[16]

In 1997, there were four federal income tax provisions *directly* aimed at assisting persons with disabilities and their families: the Medical Expense Tax Credit; the Disability Tax Credit; the Infirm Dependent Credit; and, the Attendant Care Deduction. In addition, other federal tax provisions have special rules that apply to persons with disabilities to support their participation in the workforce or in educational pursuits. As well, there are various provincial and territorial tax provisions for persons with disabilities. This section describes the four direct federal tax provisions listed above.

Medical Expense Tax Credit
The Medical Expense Tax Credit recognizes the effects of above-average medical expenses on an individual's ability to pay taxes by providing a tax credit for eligible medical expenses that are in excess of a certain percentage of the individual's net income.

In the 1996 taxation year, a person with high medical expenses could use this credit to reduce the amount of federal taxes they owed. The claimant could deduct from their taxes an amount equal to 17 per cent of qualifying un-reimbursed medical expenses, up to a maximum of three per cent of their net income, or $1,614, whichever was lower.[17] When provincial taxes were taken into account, the credit provided tax relief for about 27 per cent of eligible medical expenses, depending on the province.

The 1997 federal budget proposed an additional credit for low-income earners who incur high medical expenses. The government stated that this new refundable medical expense credit would supplement the existing credit by covering the lessor of $500 or 25 per cent of eligible medical expenses. It would be available to those with earnings above $2,500 and would be reduced by five per cent of net family income in excess of $16,069.

39

In 1996, about 1.2 million individuals claimed the Medical Expense Tax Credit. In that year, the credit was estimated to have cost the federal government about $320 million in foregone tax revenues and the provinces an additional $186 million.

Disability Tax Credit

The Disability Tax Credit recognizes the effects of a severe and prolonged impairment on an individual's ability to pay taxes. It is available to persons with a severe and prolonged mental or physical impairment that markedly restricts their ability to perform basic activities of daily life. To be eligible, an applicant's condition must be certified by a medical doctor. The Disability Tax Credit is non-refundable.

On average, the Disability Credit was worth $1,143 in federal and provincial tax savings in the 1996 tax year.[18] In that year, 577,000 individuals claimed the credit at an estimated cost of $309 million in foregone tax revenues for the federal government, plus an additional $179 million for the provinces.

Infirm Dependent Credit

Persons who care for a dependant over the age of 19 with an infirmity are eligible for the Infirm Dependent Credit. For the 1996 taxation year, the maximum federal-provincial tax savings from this provision was approximately $635 (up from about $427 in 1995).[19] That same year, the maximum credit was reduced gradually once the applicant's income exceeded $4,103. Approximately 40,000 people claimed the Infirm Dependent Tax Credit in 1996.

For the 1996 taxation year, the cost to the federal government in foregone revenue as a result of the Infirm Dependent Tax Credit was estimated to be $56 million, and the cost to the provinces was about $32 million.

Attendant Care Deduction

For persons with disabilities who require attendant care in order to work, additional tax relief is provided through the Attendant Care Deduction. This provision allows persons with disabilities to deduct up to $5,000 in eligible expenses or two-thirds of their earned income for the year, whichever is less. (The 1997 federal budget proposed removing this limit and allowing the full amount of eligible expenses to be claimed.) The actual value of the Attendant Care Deduction to an applicant depends on their tax bracket. About 450 individuals claimed the Attendant Care Deduction in the 1996 taxation year.

Benefits for Veterans

There are several different programs for war veterans in Canada.[20] Benefits under these programs are intended to recognize the contributions made by Canadians who served their country during periods of war or peacetime.

Veterans Disability Pension

Veterans of the Canadian Armed Forces, the Merchant Navy, and current and former members of the Regular or Reserve Force who suffer from a service-related medical condition may apply for a Veterans Disability Pension. The amount of pension awarded depends on the extent of disability suffered, and it is based on rates established in the Pension Act.[21] It is not dependent on the applicant's income or assets. To receive disability benefits, interested persons must apply to Veterans' Affairs Canada.

As part of the Veterans Disability Pension program, survivor benefits are available for eligible widowed spouses and children of veterans. In cases where a surviving spouse's resources are insufficient to cover the funeral expenses for the veteran, additional support may be provided. If a deceased pensioner is deemed to have died from a condition related to their military

41

service, funeral expenses are covered, regardless of the survivor's resources or the value of the veteran's estate.

In 1997, 151,000 people received benefits under the Veterans Disability Pension program, at a cost of approximately $1.1 billion.[22]

Veterans Allowance

Some veterans and civilians are eligible for the Veterans Allowance. The value of this Allowance depends on the recipient's income, marital status, and the number of dependants. In order to qualify, male applicants must be over the age of 60, and female applicants must be at least 55. In some cases of hardship, however, benefits can be provided at an earlier age.

The Veterans Allowance is an income-tested benefit, and most sources of income – such as federal retirement benefits and the Veterans Pension – are considered when determining its value. However, recipients are afforded a small earnings exemption, below which outside sources of income do not affect the size of the allowance.

In 1997, 23,000 people received the Veterans Allowance, at a cost of approximately $62 million that year.[23]

Veterans Independence Program

The Veterans Independence Program is designed to assist veterans in maintaining an independent lifestyle in their home by covering the costs of such services as grounds maintenance, housekeeping, personal care, transportation for social activities, and nursing home care.

In 1997, about 76,000 veterans received assistance under the Veterans Independence Program. The cost of this assistance, plus other related health costs for recipients of the Veterans Disability Pension and the Veterans Allowance, was estimated to have been about $600 million.

Goods and Services Tax Credit

The GST Credit is designed to reduce the impact of the GST on low-income households.[24] The amount of the credit depends on family size and income. In 1997, the basic adult credit was $199 a year. Eligible single adults, including single parents, received an addition maximum of $105. Low-income families with children received $105 a year for each child under the age of 18. The exception to this general rule allows single parents to claim the adult basic credit for one dependent child. GST Credits are reduced once family income exceeds $25,921 a year.

About 8.7 million people claim the GST Credit.[25] In the 1996 taxation year, the GST Credit cost the federal government an estimated $2.9 billion in foregone revenue. The GST Credit is refundable.

Endnotes

1. Information for this section was taken from: Dennis Guest, *The Emergence of Social Security in Canada* (Vancouver: British Columbia Press, 1985); and, *The 1995 Budget and Block Funding* (Ottawa: National Council of Welfare, Spring 1995).

2. See Guest, *The Emergence of Social Security*, pp. 1-3.

3. Information provided by the Social Program Information and Analysis Division, Strategic Policy Branch, at Human Resources Development Canada.

4. Information provided by the Social Program Information and Analysis Division, Strategic Policy Branch, at Human Resources Development Canada.

5. Unless otherwise indicated, the information for this section was taken from unpublished work by Gilles Séquin of the Social Program Information and Analysis Division at Human Resources Development Canada (Mr. Séguin was the principal researcher for *Welfare Incomes 1995* and *Another Look at Welfare Reform,* during a secondment to the National Council of Welfare in 1996-7), and from *Monitoring the Impacts on Social Assistance Recipients of Welfare Cuts and Changes: An Overview* (Ottawa: National Anti-Poverty Organization, October 1996).

6. Information provided by the Social Program Information and Analysis Division, Strategic Policy Branch, at Human Resources Development Canada.

7. Information provided by the Social Program Information and Analysis Division, Strategic Policy Branch, at Human Resources Development Canada.

8. Territorial Formula Financing is a federal transfer to the territories to help finance the costs of social assistance and social services. It is separate from the CHST.

9. For more information, contact the federal department of Indian and Northern Affairs Canada.

10. "Mobility rights" in this context refers to the right of all Canadians to access basic income supports in any part of the country. This provision prohibits the imposition of "residency requirements" such as the three-month waiting period for new residents to British Columbia that was introduced in 1995. This clause was brought in by the BC government in direct contravention of the CAP, but was dropped in the spring of 1997 following an agreement with the federal government.

11. Persons with disabilities will receive support under a separate plan administered by the provincial government, called the *Ontario Disability Support Plan*.

12. When the applicant has fixed assets in excess of the allowable non-exempt asset limit, they may be required to dispose of any excess property as a condition of their eligibility for social assistance benefits. The income generated from the sale of fixed assets is included in the calculation of the applicant's income and is deducted from the social assistance benefits paid.

13. These changes coincide with similar provisions introduced in the federal Employment Insurance program in the early 1990s that reduced, then eliminated EI benefits for applicants who quit their job "without just cause" or were dismissed from the job.

14. The assumptions used in the National Council of Welfare's report also apply to this comparison: the rates are for the largest municipal areas; the child in the one-parent family is two years of age and the children in the two-parent family are 10 and 15 years old; short-term rates of assistance are assigned to single employable individuals and couples with children; the rates for single parents are based on the employability classifications in each province; all recipients are tenants in the private rental market, and there is no sharing of accommodation. Where shelter allowances do not include the cost of utilities, the latter is added to shelter rates; maximum shelter rates are used. It is assumed that client households started receiving welfare on January 1, 1997 and will remain on assistance throughout the entire calendar year.

15.   Note that Manitoba's Child Related Income Support Program (CRISP) and Saskatchewan's Family Income Plan (FIP) are not included in this comparison because the benefits under these programs reduce, rather than supplement, the amount payable under social assistance. See Chapter 1 for a description of these programs.

16.   This section was based on information provided by the federal Department of Finance. Provincial cost estimates of tax expenditures were calculated at 58 per cent of the relevant federal costs.

17.   Among the qualifying medical expenses were the following: medical, dental, and hospital services; attendant or nursing home care; personal transportation for medical care; medical devices; necessary home renovations; and, prescription drugs.

18.   To calculate the maximum federal and provincial tax savings from the Disability Tax Credit, the Disability Amount of $4,233 (as identified on the 1996 General Tax Form) was multiplied by the 17 per cent federal credit rate, plus provincial tax savings. The average provincial tax rate in 1996 was 58 per cent of the federal rate, making the joint federal-provincial rate approximately 27 per cent; hence, the maximum credit of $1,143.

19.   The 1996 maximum was calculated by multiplying $2,353 (the Infirm Dependent Amount) by 27 per cent (the average federal-provincial credit rate). The 1995 maximum was calculated by multiplying the 1995 Infirm Dependent Amount of $1,583 by 27 per cent.

20.   Unless otherwise stated, information for this section was taken from the following pamphlets : "Veterans Services and Benefits" (Ottawa: Veterans Affairs Canada, 1996); "War Veterans Allowance," (Ottawa: Veterans Affairs Canada, 1996); and, "Veterans Disability Pensions," (Ottawa: Veterans Affairs Canada, 1997). The number of recipients of various benefits and the program costs are based on figures provided by Veterans Affairs Canada.

21.   Individuals may contact Veterans Affairs Canada for a detailed rate schedule for Veterans Disability Pensions.

22.   Based on data for March, 1997.

23.   Based on data for March, 1997.

24. Unless otherwise indicated, information for this section, including federal cost estimates, was taken from *Tax Expenditures* (Ottawa: Department of Finance Canada, 1997).

25. *Taxation Statistics on Individuals - Tax Year 1995* (Ottawa: Revenue Canada, 1997).

Chapter 3
Earnings Replacement

There are two major programs in Canada designed to insure the earnings of the working-age population: the Employment Insurance (EI) program offered by the federal government and the Workers' Compensation programs offered by the provinces. The Canada and Quebec Pension Plans, in addition to providing pensions for seniors, also provide disability and death benefits for working-age contributors. Those benefits are outlined in Chapter 4.

Employment Insurance

Background

Employment Insurance, previously called Unemployment Insurance (UI), dates back to 1941. Before the federal UI program was introduced, government assistance to unemployed workers was under the jurisdiction of the provinces. At that time, "relief" programs were delivered piecemeal at the local level. This system came under tremendous strain during the depths of the Depression, as provincial and local governments struggled to deal with widespread unemployment and social disruption.[1]

In 1941, the federal government obtained the unanimous consent of the provinces to amend the Constitution, making

47

way for the introduction of the first national Unemployment Insurance program. The original UI program was relatively limited in scope. It covered mainly urban workers in industry and commerce and provided benefits that replaced approximately half of average earnings. Less than half the workforce was included under the provisions of the original act, but the stage was set for several decades of expansion.[2]

Over the next 30 years, numerous amendments to the UI legislation expanded eligibility and improved benefit levels. In the 1940s, 1950s, and 1960s, new categories of workers were added to the plan. During the 1960s in particular, when there was a general social policy trend in Canada towards improved income supports, there were substantial changes to UI contribution and benefit levels. By the late 1960s, successive reforms had expanded UI coverage to include two-thirds of the working population.

In 1971, a broad range of reforms was introduced in "the first complete revision (of UI) since the program's inception."[3] The 1971 reforms expanded UI to cover virtually the entire work-force, increased benefit levels, expanded the benefit period, and reduced the number of weeks of work necessary to qualify for benefits, particularly for workers in regions with high unemployment. New maternity and sickness benefits were also introduced, and provisions were made to accommodate seasonal workers.

In the following years, higher unemployment rates, economic restructuring, and improved benefits led to a rapid escalation in the costs of the program. By the late 1970s, with the federal government facing annual deficits and poor economic conditions, the thrust of social policy shifted from program expansion and enhancement to cost reduction. Since then, UI amendments have increasingly restricted eligibility and benefits.[4]

During the first half of the 1990s, a series of changes was introduced which substantially reduced the cost and scope of the program. In 1990, the federal government ceased making financial contributions to UI, leaving the program to be self-funded by employees and employers. At the same time, the government increased the number of weeks of work required to receive benefits, reduced the maximum duration of benefits for workers in most regions, and reduced and later eliminated benefits for those who declined "suitable employment," quit "without just cause," or were dismissed from their job.

In 1996, the Unemployment Insurance program went through another set of comprehensive reforms as the federal government replaced the long-standing *Unemployment* Insurance program with a new *Employment* Insurance system.

The Current Employment Insurance Program

Employment Insurance (EI) is one of Canada's key income security programs. Administered by the federal government, the program provides partial earnings replacement and other supports to Canadians who are unable to work because of a job loss, temporary illness, or a period of maternity leave. Almost every person designated as an employee in the labour force contributes a portion of their earnings to the Employment Insurance fund. Employers also make contributions on behalf of their employees. The self-employed neither contribute to, nor receive benefits from, the Employment Insurance program.

In 1996, approximately 13.1 million Canadians or about 90 per cent of the labour force made EI contributions.[5] Employers and employees paid almost $19 billion into the EI fund that year. In total, $13 billion was paid out in benefits to 2.8 million recipients. On average, 911,000 Canadians received EI benefits in any given month during 1996.[6]

49

Benefits provided through the Employment Insurance program are divided into two main categories: income benefits and employment benefits.

Income Benefits

The following section outlines the main components of the income benefits package in the Employment Insurance program.[7] In 1996, each of these components was substantially restructured as a result of the change from using weeks as the basis for determining workers' EI contributions, their eligibility, and benefits, to using hours instead.

Contributions

Almost every paid employee in Canada makes EI contributions based on their earnings, up to an annual "Maximum Insurable Earnings" (MIE). In 1997, the MIE was $39,000. Prior to the 1996 changes, employees made EI contributions on, and were insured for, only the weeks when they had worked more than 15 hours or had earned more than $183. The annual MIE was $42,380.

In 1997, with an employee EI contribution rate of $2.90 per $100 of earnings, workers who earned more than the MIE paid an annual maximum of $1,131 to the EI fund.[8] The federal government refunds the EI contributions of those who earn less than $2,000 a year via the tax system.[9]

Employers also make EI contributions on behalf of their employees. In 1997, employers paid $4.06 per $100 in employee earnings, for a maximum of $1,583 per employee per year (4.06 per cent x $39,000).[10] The federal government's New Hires Program, announced in November 1996, reduced EI contributions for small businesses that created new jobs. Under this program, firms that made a total of $60,000 in EI contributions in 1996, and that paid at least $250 more in EI premiums in 1997 than in 1996, were eligible for an EI refund of up to $10,000 from the federal government (see Table 2).

The New Hires Program will be available in 1998, but the refund calculation formula will be less generous than it was in 1997.[11]

Table 2

New Hires Program – Refund Calculation Formula
The formula for calculating the 1997 refund was as follows: 1997 EI contributions – (1996 contributions + $250)   =   amount of refund to a maximum of $10,000
The formula for calculating the 1998 benefit will be as follows: (1998 EI contributions – [1996 contributions +$250]) X 25% = amount of refund to a maximum of $10,000

Source: *New Hires Program* (Ottawa: Human Resources Development, 1997, p. 6).

Eligibility

In order to qualify for benefits, workers who pay EI premiums must show that they have worked a minimum number of hours over the preceding 52 weeks or since their last EI claim.[12] This minimum varies according to the regional unemployment rate (see Table 3), starting at 420 hours in regions with very high unemployment, and rising to 700 hours in areas where unemployment is much lower. The shift from the original weeks-based system – which required employees to have participated in 12 to 20 weeks of work, depending on their regional unemployment rate – disguised a substantial increase in the number of hours required for part-time workers (those working less than 35 hours a week) to qualify for EI benefits. At the same time, it reduced the number of hours required for those working more than 35 hours a week.[13]

Table 3

EI Minimum Entrance Requirements	
Regional rate of unemployment	Required hours of insurable employment
Less than 6%	700
6.1 - 7%	665
7.1 - 8%	630
8.1 - 9%	595
9.1 - 10%	560
10.1 - 11%	525
11.1 - 12%	490
12.1 - 13%	455
More than 13%	420

Source: *Employment Insurance: Regular Benefits* (Ottawa: Human Resources Development Canada, January 1997, p. 7).

Those entering the workforce for the first time or those re-entering the labour market after an absence of two or more years are required to meet an even higher entrance requirement. Claimants in this group must work at least 910 hours in a year before they qualify for EI benefits. The stated logic behind this longer qualifying period for 'new entrants' and 're-entrants' is to discourage these individuals from "beginning a pattern of reliance on the system for regular income support [by requiring them] to show a longer attachment to the workforce."[14]

Regular Benefits

EI contributors who wish to make a claim for benefits can do so at their local Human Resources Development Centre of Canada. Under most circumstances, claimants are not permitted to receive EI benefits for periods when they are outside the country. With few exceptions, there is also a two-week waiting period for all claimants during which benefits are not paid. The first EI cheque is received usually about four weeks after an application has been made. EI claimants can apply for provincial social assistance benefits during this waiting period, but to avoid duplication, social assistance payments are automatically deducted from EI cheques once payments have begun.[15]

EI contributors who quit their job "without just cause" or are dismissed because of misconduct are not eligible for EI benefits. Human Resources Development Canada lists a number of circumstances deemed to be "just cause," such as sexual harassment, discrimination, or dangerous working conditions.[16]

The EI benefit level is calculated using a two-part process. First, the claimant's average earnings are determined by dividing their total earnings during their last 26 weeks of work by either the number of weeks they had worked during those 26 weeks, or by the so-called "minimum divisor," whichever is greater (see Table 4). The average of their earnings over the period is then multiplied by the standard earnings replacement rate, ranging from 50 to 55 per cent, to arrive at their weekly EI benefit. (The replacement rate can be increased for low-income claimants with one or more dependants, based on the Family Supplement.) In 1997, the maximum weekly benefit was $413. Claimants cannot receive EI benefits while they are receiving severance, vacation, or separation pay from their former employer.

Table 4

EI Divisor Table	
Regional rate of unemployment	Minimum divisor (in weeks)
Less than 6%	22
6.1 - 7%	21
7.1 - 8%	20
8.1 - 9%	19
9.1 - 10%	18
10.1 - 11%	17
11.1 - 12%	16
12.1 - 13%	15
More than 13%	14

Source: *Employment Insurance: Regular Benefits* (Ottawa: Human Resources Development Canada, January 1997, p. 11).

While an individual collects EI benefits, they are expected to be available for work and engaged in an active job search. In order to continue to receive benefits, they must record their job-search activities on a biweekly report card for claimants that is provided by the Human Resources Development Centre of Canada. The maximum period that an individual can collect EI benefits varies from 14 to 45 weeks, depending on the claimant's hours of work and the unemployment rate in their region (see Appendix 2 for a full breakdown). This upper limit of 45 weeks was lowered in 1996 from a 50-week maximum.

In addition to their regular EI benefits, some low-income claimants with children under the age of 18 are also eligible for the Family Supplement (FS).[17] The differential earnings replacement rate (of 60 per cent instead of the standard 55 per cent) for low-income claimants with children was replaced by the Family Supplement as part of the 1996 reforms. All EI claimants who receive the federal Child Tax Benefit (CTB) and meet the low-income family eligibility criteria can receive the Family Supplement. It is paid biweekly as part of the EI cheque, and its value mirrors that of the recipient's monthly CTB (prorated to biweekly), but subject to some additional limitations that do not apply to the CTB.

Only EI claimants with family incomes below $20,921 were eligible for the maximum Family Supplement in 1997.[18] (Eligibility for the Family Supplement is based on family income from the previous tax year.) Claimants with family incomes between $20,921 and $25,921 received a partial FS, which falls by two per cent for each $100 above $20,921. In 1997, the maximum combination of regular EI benefits plus the FS was 65 per cent of a claimant's average insurable earnings. This maximum will rise by five percentage points each year until the year 2000, at which time it will reach a ceiling of 80 per cent.[19] The combined regular EI benefit plus the FS cannot exceed the standard EI benefit maximum of $413 a week.

Table 5

EI Earnings Exemption		
Weekly EI benefits	Allowable earnings	Total weekly income
$50	$50	$100
$100	$50	$150
$150	$50	$200
$200	$50	$250
$201	25% of EI benefits	

Source: *A 21st Century Employment System for Canada: Guide to the Employment Insurance Legislation* (Ottawa: Human Resources Development Canada, December 1995, p. 17).

Low-income claimants are also permitted to retain work earnings of up to $50 a week or 25 per cent of their weekly EI benefit amount, whichever is greater (see Table 5).[20] This "earnings exemption" was designed to encourage low-income EI recipients to accept part-time or temporary work that might lead to greater employment opportunities, thereby reducing the need for future EI support.

People with annual incomes above $48,750 who receive EI benefits must pay back 30 per cent or more of the money they received in benefits. Prior to the 1996 changes, this high-income claw-back applied only to those with incomes above $63,570. [21]

On average, there were more than 700,000 claimants receiving regular EI benefits each month in 1996. The EI fund paid out a total of $9.6 billion in regular benefits that year.[22]

Penalties for Repeat Claimants

In 1996, an "intensity rule" was introduced with the other EI changes. It has the effect of reducing payments for all claimants who have received more than 20 weeks of EI benefits over the previous five years. The basic reduction rate for repeat claimants is set at one per cent for each additional 20 weeks of EI benefits over the last five years, up to a maximum of five percentage points off the standard earnings replacement rate of 55 per cent (see Table 6). The intensity rule only takes into account the number of weeks of regular benefits claimed since June 1996, meaning that it will take until the year 2001 for the maximum five percentage-point penalty to be fully in effect. Low-income claimants who are eligible for the Family Supplement are exempt from the intensity rule provisions.

Under the intensity rule, for each year that an EI contributor is claim free, lost percentage points from the earnings replacement rate are reinstated, up to the maximum of 55 per cent. EI recipients can also reduce potential future intensity-rule penalties by finding work while they collect EI benefits. Individuals who work while on claim and earn enough to reduce their weekly EI benefit cheque are given a "credit" against future intensity-rule penalties. For example, if a claimant's EI benefit cheque is reduced by half because of income

Table 6

Intensity Rule for Repeat EI Claimants		
Number of weeks of EI benefits in the last 5 years	Earnings replacement rate penalty	Earnings replacement rate
0 - 20	0%	55%
21 - 40	1%	54%
41 - 60	2%	53%
61 - 80	3%	52%
81 - 100	4%	51%
More than 100	5%	50%

Source: *Employment Insurance: Regular Benefits* (Ottawa: Human Resources Development Canada, January 1997, p. 13).

Table 7

EI Repeat User Claw-back for Higher-income Earners	
Number of weeks of EI benefits in the past 5 years	Maximum portion of EI benefits that can be taxed back
21 - 40	50%
41 - 60	60%
61 - 80	70%
81 - 100	80%
101 - 120	90%
Over 120	100%

Source: *A 21st Century Employment System for Canada: Guide to the Employment Insurance Legislation* (Ottawa: Human Resources Development Canada, December 1995, p. 13).

they have earned while on claim, only half of the weeks of their claim are recorded in their benefit history.[23]

Repeat claimants with earnings above the MIE of $39,000 are subject to the intensity rule, plus an additional penalty.[24] From these individuals, EI benefits are clawed back at an accelerated rate, ranging from 50 to 100 per cent of their total EI benefits in a given year, depending on their claims history (see Table 7).

Special Benefits

Some EI contributors are also eligible for "special benefits" for sickness, maternity, and parental leave.[25] To be eligible for these benefits, claimants must have worked for 700 hours over the previous 52 weeks or since their last EI claim. Sickness benefits are paid for a maximum of 15 weeks. Natural mothers are also eligible for 15 weeks of maternity benefits. An additional 10 weeks of parental benefits can be shared between the mother and father. In cases where special care is required due to the ill health of a newborn, an additional five weeks of parental benefits can be claimed. Adoptive parents are eligible for both the standard 10 weeks of parental benefits, plus the additional five weeks, where applicable.

The earnings replacement rate for special benefits is the standard 55 per cent. Some low-income claimants are also eligible for the Family Supplement. As well, special benefits claimants are subject to the regular (30 per cent) high-income claw-back if their annual income exceeds the $48,750 threshold. However, they are not subject to the intensity rule provisions regarding repeat claimants. Unlike regular EI beneficiaries, people receiving special benefits are not expected to look for work.

There were an average of 35,000 people receiving sickness benefits during any month in 1996, plus another 84,000 recipients claiming maternity, parental, or adoption benefits. Sickness benefits paid that year totalled $450 million, with another $1.3 billion paid in maternity, parental, and adoption benefits.

Fishing Benefits

In general, the self-employed neither contribute to, nor benefit from, Employment Insurance. Self-employed people who fish for a livelihood, however, do pay EI contributions and they are eligible for fishing benefits provided that they meet the entrance requirements.[26] Unlike regular benefits, eligibility for fishing benefits is calculated according to earnings, rather than hours worked. Entrance requirements vary according to the regional unemployment rates (see Table 8).

Table 8

EI Fishing Benefits Entrance Requirements	
Regional unemployment rate	Earnings
6% and under	$4,200
6.1 - 7%	$4,000
7.1 - 8%	$3,800
8.1 - 9%	$3,600
9.1 - 10%	$3,400
10.1 - 11%	$3,200
11.1 - 12%	$2,900
12.1 - 13%	$2,700
13.1 and over	$2,500

Source: *Employment Insurance and Fishing* (Ottawa: Human Resources Development Canada, 1997, p. 3).

People who fish for a living in areas with very high unemployment rates can qualify for benefits with earnings as low as $2,500 over the qualifying period (a maximum of 31 weeks prior to filing a claim). The entrance requirement rises to $4,200 in earnings in regions with very low unemployment. New entrants and re-entrants must earn at least $5,500 during the qualifying period before receiving benefits, irrespective of their regional unemployment rate.

Eligible claimants are entitled to a maximum of 26 weeks of fishing benefits that can be received either consecutively or intermittently during a maximum period of 37 to 38 weeks. Winter fishing benefits can start as early as the week of October 1, and they must end no later than the week of June 15. Summer benefits can start as early as the week of April 1 and must end no later than the week of December 15. Claimants of fishing benefits must obtain a Record of Employment from their employer, buyer or agent, and they can apply for benefits at their local Human Resources Development Centre of Canada. Fishing benefits are subject to the standard two-week waiting period. While in receipt of fishing benefits, recipients must submit their biweekly claimant's report card, and they must be actively looking for work.

Fishing benefits are calculated using a three-part process. First, the claimant's total self-employed earnings from fishing over the previous 31 weeks are divided by the regional divisor (the same divisor table used to calculate regular benefits). This figure – the claimant's average earnings from self-employed fishing – is then added to their average earnings from non-fishing work. The average for non-fishing work is calculated by dividing the total non-fishing earnings from the 26 weeks prior to filing a claim by the regional divisor. The claimant's average earnings – the sum of both average fishing and non-fishing earnings – is then multiplied by the standard EI replacement rate of 55 per cent in order to determine the weekly benefit. The maximum weekly benefit is the regular EI maximum of $413.

Fishing benefits are subject to both the intensity-rule provisions which govern regular EI benefits and the high-income claw-back rules. Low-income recipients of fishing benefits are eligible for the Family Supplement if they meet the standard requirements.

In any given month in 1996, an average of 10,000 people received fishing benefits under the Employment Insurance program. Almost $218 million in fishing benefits were paid that year.

Penalties for Fraudulent Claims

Individuals caught defrauding the Employment Insurance system are subject to a range of penalties including fines and steeper entrance requirements for future claims. If an overpayment of EI benefits is made due to undeclared earnings, the maximum penalty is three times the amount of the overpayment. In cases where the fraud was *not* due to undeclared earnings, or the claimant did not qualify for benefits, a maximum penalty of three times the weekly benefit amount can be imposed for each false claim. The government can impose higher entrance requirements for claimants with a history of violations since June 30, 1996. The severity of the penalty depends upon the seriousness of the violation (see Table 9).

Table 9

Penalties for Fraudulent EI Claims		
Value of fraud	Increase in the minimum entrance requirements	Example: 700 hours would become ...
less than $1,000	25%	875 hours
$1,000 - $4,999	50%	1,050 hours
over $5,000	75%	1,225 hours

Source: *Employment Insurance: Regular Benefits* (Ottawa: Human Resources Development Canada, January 1997, p. 22).

Employment Benefits

In addition to income available under EI, contributors to the program can also apply for a range of "employment benefits." These benefits, which are to be delivered by Human Resources Development Canada, were still in a process of transition in 1997, and they will be subject to substantial changes over the next few years. (Inquire at any Canada Human Resources Development Centre for the most up-to-date details.) At present, depending upon the province or region and the local

Human Resources Development Centre, EI contributors can apply for a range of employment benefits which include training, self-employment assistance, career counselling, job placement services, and labour market information.

When the 1996 EI reforms were introduced, the federal government announced its intention to reform the employment benefits system. At that time, it offered to negotiate bilateral agreements with the provinces and territories by 1999 that would determine the shape of these reforms.[27] These agreements will determine the nature of the supports available and the roles that the respective levels of government will play. By the end of 1997, almost all provinces and territories had concluded such agreements with the federal government.

In its offer to the provinces and territories, the federal government suggested "active measures" that could be included in the employment benefits package, including skills and loans grants, earnings supplements, employer subsidies, supports for small business start-ups, and funds for local job creation initiatives. As well, the federal government would continue to provide "labour market services" such as applicant screening and referral, career counselling, and information about job placements and the labour market. The federal government stated that it will phase out direct federal participation in training programs by 1999.

Several possible delivery mechanisms were set out by the federal government to guide the new agreements: the federal government could continue to provide both labour market services and active measures; provinces and territories could receive EI funds to deliver the programs and services themselves; or, provinces and territories could receive EI funds to deliver their own employment measures as long as they were consistent with the guidelines of the EI Act. Provinces or territories that choose to deliver the active measures could also deliver the labour market services currently handled by the federal government. Regardless of the model selected in each jurisdiction, the federal government stated that it would continue to manage national labour market information through Human Resources Development Canada.

The federal government also stated that the active measures in the employment benefits package would be made available to EI claimants and to those who have qualified for EI benefits or have established an EI claim that ended within the last three years. Individual claimants who received maternity or parental benefits within the last five years would also be eligible.

Workers' Compensation

Background

The Ontario Workers' Compensation Act of 1914 was Canada's first piece of social insurance.[28] This Act was followed by similar legislation in each province and territory. By 1930, most provinces had established workers' compensation systems. Prince Edward Island and Newfoundland introduced workers' compensation systems in 1949 and 1950 respectively, with the territories finally adopting similar programs in the early 1970s.

The Ontario workers' compensation plan and those that followed established a system of compulsory income protection against work-related sickness, disability, or death.[29] Compensation was originally paid in the form of cash assistance, with medical and rehabilitative services added later by various jurisdictions. Assistance was considered to be "no-fault," in that compensation was paid as long as the sickness, injury, or death stemmed from the workplace (except in rare cases where wilful misconduct led to non-serious injuries).

Prior to the establishment of workers' compensation in Canada, the only recourse for workers or their dependants who sought compensation for work-related illness, injury, or death was through the courts. This posed many challenges for injured workers and their families, not the least of which was the cost of accessing the court system and the long delays associated with settling claims, especially at a time when the worker was unable to earn an income through regular employment.

The greatest barrier to compensation, however, was that the courts overwhelmingly favoured the interests of employers over the rights of injured workers and their dependants. Employers were usually able to shield themselves from liability by demonstrating that the victim was in some way responsible for the injury or death, the accident was caused by the actions of a fellow employee, or that the accident resulted from normal risks associated with a particular job.

As the number of industrial accidents and deaths rose – coinciding with increased industrialization in Canada – and as more workers fought unsuccessfully for compensation from their employers, public interest in the concept of no-fault social insurance for workplace injuries and deaths became wide-spread. Increasingly, workplace accidents came to be viewed as one of the costs of industrial progress that must be shared collectively, rather than a cost to be borne by the unfortunate few who were injured while working.

Initially, businesses reacted negatively to the idea of a no-fault social insurance scheme, but they soon realized that such a system would stabilize costs and spread the risk across employers. After studying the potential costs and benefits of such a plan, the Canadian Manufacturers Association lent its support to the concept even before the first act was passed in Ontario.

Workers' Compensation Programs

Workers' compensation is designed to protect individuals against wage loss due to workplace injury or disease.[30] It is a form of social insurance by which employers share collective liability for the workers in their industry through compulsory contributions to a publicly administered plan. In exchange, workers collectively waive their right to sue their employer in the event of a work-related injury or disease. Instead, workers seek redress through the workers' compensation program in their jurisdiction.

Each province and territory in Canada operates its own workers' compensation system. The federal government covers its employees under a separate plan. Between 70 and 100 per cent of workers are covered by workers' compensation, depending on the jurisdiction.[31] Participation is generally compulsory, but some industries are exempt, such as certain small businesses, particularly in agriculture. Exempt employers can voluntarily join the workers' compensation plan in their jurisdiction, provided that they pay an annual assessment based on the size of their payroll that is required of all plan members.

In each province and territory, an autonomous agency – generally referred to as the Workers' Compensation Board (WCB) – is charged with the responsibility of administering the provincial/territorial workers' compensation act.[32] The main function of the WCB is to determine whether or not, and to what extent, a given individual is eligible for compensation. The WCB carries out this duty by communicating directly with the affected worker (or their dependants in the case of survivor claims), the employer, and other agencies from whom information is required in order to establish a claim.

In 1995, there were almost 825,000 occupational injuries reported in Canada. In that year, combined spending on workers' compensation benefits by the various WCBs across the country totalled almost $5 billion.[33]

Eligibility

Any employee working in an insured industry can apply for benefits if they are injured on the job or develop a work-related disease. When an illness or injury is deemed to have originated in the workplace, compensation is generally paid, however, there are some instances where compensation can be denied. This is the case if the injury or disease is the direct result of wilful misconduct on the part of the claimant, and the injury or disease does not result in serious disability or death.

To verify a claim, the WCB may order a worker to undergo a medical examination to determine the extent of the injury. The worker's right to compensation may be suspended if they refuse to comply with the WCB's order. In most jurisdictions, benefits commence on the day following the injury.

Benefits

Workers' compensation benefits are based on the earnings of the injured worker at the time of the accident, up to a legislated maximum, and on the extent and duration of the disability. The extent and duration of disabilities are determined through a medical examination and a disability rating schedule established by the WCB. Benefits include both cash compensation and support services. Cash compensation is paid to the injured worker for a temporary or permanent disability, or to the surviving spouse and other dependants in the case of a worker's death.

Generally speaking, compensation for a temporary disability is based on the pre-accident earnings of the worker who files the claim. In cases involving a more severe or longer-term disability, the worker's potential earnings are also considered when determining benefit levels. Claimants may also receive medical assistance and physical or vocational rehabilitation services. These services play a key role in meeting the WCB's objective of returning injured workers to suitable employment whenever possible.

Cash compensation amounts for temporary disability claims are determined by multiplying a claimant's earnings – up the maximum insurable earnings – by the earnings replacement rate. (The earnings replacement rate and the maximum insurable earnings for temporary disability claims in various jurisdictions are outlined in Table 10.[34]) Benefits are also subject to a weekly maximum, which in some jurisdictions varies for claimants with or without spouses or dependants.[35]

In most jurisdictions in Canada, the replacement rate is calculated as a percentage of the *net* earnings of a claimant prior to an injury, that is, their earnings after deductions are made for Canada or Quebec Pension Plan, Employment Insurance, and income tax. As shown in Table 10, replacement rates range from a low of 75 per cent of net earnings in Newfoundland, to a high of 90 per cent of net earnings in a number of jurisdictions, including Ontario, Quebec, Manitoba (for the first two years), Saskatchewan, Alberta, and the Northwest Territories. In British Columbia and the Yukon, benefits are calculated as a percentage of *gross* earnings, that is, earnings before any deductions are made. In both jurisdictions, the earnings replacement rate is 75 per cent.

Also shown in Table 10, the maximum insurable earnings vary substantially between jurisdictions, ranging from a low of $35,900 in PEI, to a high of $56,100 in Ontario. Earnings above this maximum level are not insured by workers' compensation.

The method of calculating compensation for permanent disability claims varies widely from one jurisdiction to the next and depends on a number of factors, including the severity of the disability, the age of the claimant, their earnings potential, and whether or not they have any dependants. In addition to – or in place of – ongoing income assistance, a number of jurisdictions provide upfront lump-sum payments to claimants

65

of permanent disability compensation.[36] Non-cash supports such as attendant or personal care are also available when required.

Table 10

Workers' Compensation, Temporary Disability Benefits: Earnings Replacement Rates and Maximum Insurable Earnings, Various Jurisdictions in Canada, 1997		
Jurisdiction	Earnings replacement rate	Maximum annual insurable earnings
Prince Edward Island	80% of net earnings for the first 39 weeks, 85% thereafter	$35,900
Newfoundland	75% of net earnings for the first 39 weeks, 80% thereafter	$45,500
Nova Scotia	75% of net earnings for the first 26 weeks, 85% thereafter	$38,600
New Brunswick	80% of loss of earnings for the first 39 weeks, 85% thereafter	$43,300
Quebec	90% of net earnings	$49,000
Ontario	90% of net earnings	$56,100
Manitoba	90% of net earnings for the first 24 months, 80% of cumulative benefits thereafter	$49,530
Saskatchewan	90% of net earnings	$48,000
Alberta	90% of net earnings	$44,700
British Columbia	75% of gross earnings	$55,800
Yukon	75% of gross earnings	$54,200
Northwest Territories	90% of net earnings	$49,000
Source: *Workers' Compensation Benefit Comparisons* (Edmonton: Association of Workers' Compensation Boards of Canada, 1997).		

Workers' compensation cash benefits are not taxable, and they are usually paid as long as the claimant is unable to return to work. A number of jurisdictions reduce the workers' compensation benefits by any amount of Canada or Quebec Pension Plan benefits received by the claimant. No other sources of income are deducted from workers' compensation benefits.

If a worker dies as a result of an injury or disease sustained in the workplace, benefits are paid to the surviving spouse and dependants. This assistance generally includes a lump-sum payment, plus ongoing benefits that are tied to the age and the employability of the surviving spouse, and the number of dependent children. In some jurisdictions, benefits are paid until the spouse remarries or dies, while other jurisdictions pay benefits even after the surviving spouse remarries. Dependent children continue to receive benefits regardless of whether or not the surviving spouse remarries.

Endnotes

1. Dennis Guest, *The Emergence of Social Security in Canada* (Vancouver: University of British Columbia Press, 1985, p. 93).

2. *CCSD Response to Bill C-12: An Act Respecting Employment Insurance in Canada* (Ottawa: Canadian Council on Social Development, April 1996, p. 33).

3. Dennis Guest, *The Emergence of Social Security in Canada* (Vancouver: University of British Columbia Press, 1985, p. 166).

4. *CCSD Response to Bill C-12: An Act Respecting Employment Insurance In Canada* (Ottawa: Canadian Council on Social Development, April 1996).

5. This figure is an estimate based on contributor data from previous years and current labour force data.

6. *Employment Insurance Statistics* (Ottawa: Statistics Canada, forthcoming).

7. Unless otherwise noted, information for this section was drawn from *Employment Insurance: Regular Benefits* (Ottawa: Human Resources Development Canada, January 1997).

8. *Budget Plan* (Ottawa: Department of Finance Canada, 1997, p. 81).

9. *A 21st Century Employment System for Canada: Guide to the Employment Insurance Legislation* (Ottawa: Human Resources Development Canada, December 1995, p. 16).

10. *Budget Plan* (Ottawa: Department of Finance Canada, 1997, p. 81).

11. *The New Hires Program* (Ottawa: Revenue Canada, 1997, pp. 4-7).

12. Those who quit their job "without just cause" or are fired are not eligible for Employment Insurance benefits.

13. *CCSD Response to Bill C-12: An Act Respecting Employment Insurance in Canada* (Ottawa: Canadian Council on Social Development, April 1996, pp. 4-5).

14. *Backgrounder* (Ottawa: Human Resources Development Canada, December 1995, p. 4).

15. *Employment Insurance and Social Assistance* (Ottawa: Human Resources Development Canada, 1996).

16. *Employment Insurance: Regular Benefits* (Ottawa: Human Resources Development Canada, January 1997, p. 16).

17. *Employment Insurance and the Family Income Supplement* (Ottawa: Human Resources Development Canada, 1997).

18. "Family income" refers to "family net income" as used for tax purposes. Net income includes earnings, interest, and other income, less any deductions such as child care expenses or RRSPs. Although not treated as taxable income, workers' compensation benefits and social assistance income are included in the net income amount.

19. Information provided by Human Resources Development Canada, 1997.

20. *A 21st Century Employment System for Canada: Guide to the Employment Insurance Legislation*, (Ottawa: Human Resources Development Canada, December 1995, pp. 16-17).

21. Ibid., pp. 13-14.

22. *Employment Insurance Statistics* (Ottawa: Statistics Canada, forthcoming).

23. "Augustine proposes Employment Insurance bill changes to strengthen work incentives while raising claimant incomes" (Ottawa: Jean Augustine, MP, *Communiqué*, March 21, 1996). This amendment to the EI legislation was later passed.

24. Ibid., pp. 13-14.

25. *Employment Insurance - Maternity, parental and sickness benefits* (Ottawa: Human Resources Development, 1997, pp. 1- 17).

26. *Employment Insurance and Fishing* (Ottawa: Human Resources Development Canada, 1997, pp. 1-13).

27. *Getting Canadians Back to Work: A Proposal to Provinces and Territories for a New Partnership in the Labour Market* (Ottawa: Human Resources Development Canada, May 1996, pp. 1-4).

28. Information for this section was taken from: Melanie Hess, *The Canadian Fact Book on Income Security Programs* (Ottawa: Canadian Council on Social Development, 1992); *Inventory of Income Security Programs in Canada* (Ottawa: Human Resources Development, January 1993); and, unpublished information from the Association of Workers' Compensation Boards of Canada.

29. Quebec was the first province to make a contribution to the workers' compensation field with its Compensation Act in 1909, but the Quebec system was non-compulsory, and it maintained the historical practice of recognizing "contributory negligence" which allowed the courts to deny compensation if an employer could show that the accident was the fault of the injured worker. It did not provide an independent tribunal to determine compensation.

30. General information about Workers' Compensation was taken from *Inventory of Income Security Programs in Canada* (Ottawa: Human Resources Development Canada, January 1993) and from Melanie Hess, *The Canadian Fact Book on Income Security Programs* (Ottawa: Canadian Council on Social Development, 1992). More detailed figures and updated program requirements were taken from *Workers' Compensation Benefit Comparisons – 1997* (Edmonton: Association of Workers' Compensation Boards of Canada, 1997).

31. Data from the Association of Workers' Compensation Boards of Canada, based on annual reports of member Workers' Compensation Boards.

32. In Quebec and Newfoundland, these agencies are referred to as "Commissions" rather than "Boards."

33. *Occupational Injuries and their cost in Canada 1991-1995* (Ottawa: Human Resources Development Canada, 1996, p. 10).

34. There are minor differences in the definitions of "net earnings" used by the various jurisdictions. The information is described here simply to provide a general

comparison. To perform a more detailed analysis, see information provided in the publication, *Workers' Compensation Benefit Comparisons – 1997*, or use information available through Workers' Compensation Boards.

35. See *Workers' Compensation Benefit Comparisons – 1997* (Edmonton: Association of Workers' Compensation Boards of Canada, 1997).

36. For more information about permanent disability amounts, see *Workers' Compensation Benefit Comparisons – 1997* (Edmonton: Association of Workers' Compensation Boards of Canada, 1997).

Chapter 4
Retirement and the Elderly

Canada's system of income security programs for retirement and the elderly consists of three main components or "pillars": federal monthly allowances to the elderly called Old Age Security; the Canada and Quebec Pension Plans which offer benefits to all who have paid into the plans; and publicly supported and regulated private savings plans such as Registered Retirement Savings Plans (RRSPs), Registered Pension Plans (RPPs) and Deferred Profit Sharing Plans (DPSPs). Taken together, these three pillars provide all Canadians with a basic level of income security in their retirement years, in addition to offering incentives to those who wish to save privately for their retirement. These programs account for the largest share of federal income security program spending for any age group. And due to the aging of Canada's population, this is also the area where federal spending is expected to rise the most in future years.

Old Age Security

Background

The roots of Canada's Old Age Security program date back to the beginning of the century when the issue of pensions for the elderly was first raised in the House of Commons.[1] After years of debate, the federal government proclaimed the Old Age Pensions Act in 1927. This Act established a national, non-contributory, means-tested pension program that was jointly funded by the federal and provincial governments.

Although this was a considerable step forward in reducing poverty among seniors, the Old Age Pensions Act was criticized for its stringent eligibility rules that made it difficult for many seniors to collect even a meagre pension. In response to public pressure for improved benefits, the federal government brought in the Old Age Security Act in 1952 which offered universal pensions to the elderly for the first time in Canada.

The Old Age Security Act introduced a two-part expansion of income supports for the elderly. For the first time, a special tax or "contribution" was levied to support the program. It made a universal pension, financed and administered by the federal government, available to *all* Canadians aged 70 or older who had lived in the country for at least 20 years. It also introduced a means-tested benefit for persons aged 65 to 69. This benefit was administered by the provinces, with the federal government paying half the costs.

In 1967, the federal government introduced the Guaranteed Income Supplement (GIS). The GIS was an income-tested benefit designed to provide a minimum level of income support to recipients of Old Age Security (OAS) who were not eligible for benefits under the Canada or Quebec Pension Plans that had been established a year earlier. The age of eligibility for OAS benefits was lowered gradually between 1966 and 1970, from 70 to 65 years. This combination of OAS, GIS, and the CPP/QPP have contributed to a substantial decline in the poverty rate among seniors since the 1960s.

In 1975, the Old Age Security Act was amended to include a new income-tested benefit – the Spouse's Allowance (SPA) – for spouses of OAS pensioners who were too young to be eligible for OAS or GIS in their own right. Originally, the SPA was paid only to spouses of living OAS pensioners, but legislative changes in 1979 and 1985 extended benefits to all widows between the ages of 60 and 64, whether their spouses had collected OAS benefits or not.[2] Upon turning 65, these individuals became eligible to receive OAS in their own right.

The universality of OAS pensions ended in 1989, when the federal government began clawing back benefits through the tax system. All senior citizens still received their regular OAS benefit cheque, but those with higher incomes repaid some or all of their OAS benefits to the federal government when they filed their income taxes.[3]

The Current Old Age Security System

The old age security system provides all seniors in Canada with a guaranteed minimum income. It is designed to replace a substantial portion of preretirement income, particularly for modest and middle-income earners. Old age benefits are paid by the federal government from general government revenues.

The old age security system consists of the Old Age Security (OAS) pension, the Guaranteed Income Supplement (GIS), and the Spouse's Allowance (SPA). Although benefits are income-tested, almost all seniors receive some money from one or more old age security program because few seniors have private incomes substantial enough to make them ineligible for support.[4] In 1996, the federal government spent $21.5 billion in benefits for programs in the old age security system.[5]

Old Age Security Pension

Most seniors rely on the OAS pension for their basic income.[6] The benefit is paid monthly to persons aged 65 years and older who meet the necessary eligibility requirements. To receive OAS, individuals must apply to the Income Security Branch of Human Resources Development Canada. It is recommended that persons apply six months before becoming eligible, although one can apply as early as one year in advance.

To qualify for an OAS pension, a person must be aged 65 or older and a Canadian citizen or legal resident of Canada. Those who have at least 40 years' residency in Canada after the age of 18 are eligible for a full OAS pension.[7] Partial OAS pensions are paid at a rate of one-fortieth of a full pension for each year of Canadian residence.[8] Seniors living in Canada must have been residents for at least 10 years after the age of 18 in order to be eligible for a partial OAS pension. For those living outside of Canada, the residency requirement is 20 years.[9] However, persons from countries that have signed social security agreements with the Canadian government may be eligible for OAS pension benefits with less than the standard residency requirements.

OAS pension benefits are not based on past contributions or earnings. They are paid to individuals who meet the eligibility requirements listed above, but are taxed back from those with higher incomes. Until recently, OAS recipients with higher incomes were required to repay the benefits when they filed their income tax returns. In July 1996, the procedures were changed so that now, the reduction is removed directly from the monthly benefits cheques of high-income OAS recipients.[10] In 1997, the reduction rate was 15 cents for each dollar in annual income above $53,215.[11] OAS benefits are eliminated once an individual's annual income reaches approximately $85,000.

In 1997, the maximum monthly OAS benefit was $406, or $4,876 per year; couples received up to $812 per month, for a total of $9,752 per year. OAS benefits are taxable and fully indexed to inflation. They are adjusted quarterly to match changes in the Consumer Price Index. In 1996, approximately 3.5 million Canadians received OAS pension benefits each month, costing the federal government $16.4 billion over the year.[12]

Guaranteed Income Supplement

The Guaranteed Income Supplement (GIS) is paid monthly to low-income OAS recipients.[13] It is calculated according to the individual's income, or in the case of married couples, it is based on the incomes of both spouses. Each year, OAS recipients must reapply for the GIS because the amount of the benefit is dependent upon family income from the previous year. Unlike OAS, GIS payments are not taxable. GIS benefits are paid for up to six months after a recipient leaves Canada.

In 1997, single GIS recipients were eligible for a maximum monthly benefit of $483, or $5,795 per year. For couples, where both partners were OAS pensioners, the maximum GIS was $629 per month or $7,549 per year in 1997. OAS recipients who have no other sources of income receive the maximum amount. In 1997, the GIS was reduced by 50 cents for each dollar of family income other than OAS.[14]

In 1996, 1.3 million Canadians received the Guaranteed Income Supplement each month, accounting for 37 per cent of all OAS pensioners, at a cost of $4.6 billion to the federal government that year.[15]

Spouse's Allowance

The Spouse's Allowance (SPA) is a benefit designed to improve the financial security of widowed persons and couples who are living on the pension of only one spouse.[16] It is a monthly benefit paid to spouses of GIS recipients and to widows or widowers between the ages of 60 and 64.

To qualify for the SPA, an applicant must have lived in Canada for at least 10 years after the age of 18. They must be a Canadian citizen or a legal resident of Canada. Recipients of the SPA are required to reapply for benefits each year, and payments are made until the recipient reaches age 65. Like the GIS, the SPA is payable for up to six months after a recipient leaves Canada. Couples receiving the SPA are no longer eligible for the benefit if they separate or divorce. As well, widows or widowers who remarry are generally no longer eligible for the SPA.

The SPA is an income-tested benefit based on family or combined spousal income.[17] The maximum benefit for the spouse of a GIS recipient is equal to the combined OAS benefit and the maximum GIS at the married rate – which was $721 a month or $8,651 per year in 1997. For a widow, the amount was somewhat higher at $796 per month or $9,550 per year.

The Spouse's Allowance is non-taxable and, like the Old Age Security pension and the Guaranteed Income Supplement, it is adjusted quarterly to accommodate changes in the Consumer Price Index. In 1996, approximately 101,000 Canadians received the Spouse's Allowance each month, at a cost of $398 million for the year.[18]

Provincial Supplements for Seniors

Provincial and territorial governments in Ontario, Manitoba, Saskatchewan, Alberta, British Columbia, the Yukon, and the Northwest Territories provide senior citizens with income supplements in addition to the federal benefits. In 1997, approximately 250,000 senior citizens received provincial or territorial income supplements at a cost of about $285 million. Generally, senior citizens in some provinces also have access to a range of other provincial or territorial supports, including health and prescription drug coverage, shelter allowances, and property tax rebates.[19]

In each of the jurisdictions mentioned, senior citizens who receive federal income supports also receive income supplements, as long as they meet the provincial or territorial means or income tests and the residency requirements. The supplements are administered in conjunction with the provincial or territorial social assistance benefits. They are paid monthly, except in Manitoba, where payments are made quarterly. Unlike federal benefits to the elderly, the provincial and territorial supplements generally are not tied to inflation. For this reason, the real value of these supplements has declined over the years. Table 11 summarizes the maximum benefits that were available in 1997 in each jurisdiction.[20]

Table 11

Provincial/Territorial Supplements for the Elderly, 1997		
	Maximum Annual Benefit ($)	
	Single person	Two-pension couple
Ontario GAINS-A	996	1,992
Manitoba 55 Plus	447	959
Saskatchewan Income Plan	1,080	1,740
Alberta Seniors Benefits	2,350	3,500
British Columbia GAIN	592	1,446
Yukon Senior's Income Supplement	1,200	2,400
Northwest Territories Senior Citizens' Benefits	1,620	3,240
Source: Social Program Information and Analysis Directorate, Social Policy Branch, Strategic Policy Group, Human Resources Development Canada, 1997.		

Tax Benefits for Senior Citizens

The income tax system also provides many senior citizens with additional assistance.[21] In 1997, there were two non-refundable tax credits targeted to senior citizens: the Age Credit and the Pension Income Credit.

The Age Credit is available to individual taxpayers aged 65 and older. For the 1996 taxation year, a maximum credit of approximately $935 (depending on the province) was available to senior citizens with incomes of $25,921 or less.[22] Senior citizens with incomes above this amount were eligible for a reduced credit, provided that their incomes did not exceed $49,134, at which point the credit disappeared.[23] Since the Age Credit is non-refundable, senior citizens cannot use it to reduce their taxable income below zero. However, they can transfer any unused portion of the credit to their spouse.[24]

The Pension Income Credit is available to individuals who report private pension or annuity income in a given tax year.[25] The maximum credit was approximately $270 for the 1996 taxation year, depending on the province.[26] In 1996, the maximum credit was paid to individuals who reported pension or annuity income of at least $1,000. Like the Age Credit, the Pension Income Credit is non-refundable, and any unused portion can be transferred to a spouse.[27]

About three million Canadians claim the Age Credit, and two million claim the Pension Income Credit.[28] The Age Credit cost the federal government $1.3 billion in foregone tax revenues for the 1996 taxation year, plus $750 million in foregone revenues for the provinces. The Pension Income Credit accounted for another $350 million in foregone federal revenues and $200 million in foregone provincial revenues that same year.[29]

The Proposed Seniors Benefit

In its 1996 budget, the federal government proposed major changes to the old age security system that would reduce its costs in the future.[30] The announced changes – which still required legislative approval at the end of 1997 – would roll back, and in some cases eliminate, support for higher-income seniors, and would increase modestly the benefits for very low-income senior citizens. For the federal government, the net result of these changes would be a substantial reduction in the cost of providing basic income support for seniors, just as members of the large baby-boom generation start to retire.

If the proposed changes are passed, the Old Age Security pension will be combined with the Guaranteed Income

Supplement in 2001 to become the new Seniors Benefit. The Age Credit and Pension Income Credit which seniors receive through the income tax system would also become part of the new benefit, while the Spouse's Allowance would continue as a separate benefit. Canadians over the age of 60 as of December 31, 1995, would have the choice of moving to the new system or staying with their current benefit structure for the rest of their lives.[31] Anyone under this age would automatically fall under the new system.

The proposed Seniors Benefit is intended to be a tax-free, income-tested benefit paid to all eligible Canadians over the age of 65. It need not be reported on income tax returns and would not be considered when calculating refundable tax credits. Seniors would be required to apply for the benefit upon turning 65 years old, but would receive benefits automatically each following year, with the benefit level calculated according to their previous year's tax return. The proposed new benefit would maintain the residency requirements of the current OAS pension.

The new benefit would also be fully indexed to inflation. And, unlike the current system, the income thresholds used to determine the maximum benefit would also be indexed to inflation so that their real value would not erode over time.

The Seniors Benefit would be paid monthly, and it would be based on family or combined spousal income, rather than individual income. (The current OAS reduction is calculated on individual income, while the GIS is based on family or combined spousal income.) In the case of couples, it would mean that the size of their benefit would vary according to their combined income, although equal cheques would be paid to each spouse.

Table 12

The Proposed Seniors Benefit, 2001 (in 1996 $)		
Annual income from other sources [1] ($)	Seniors Benefit (annual payment)	
	Singles	Couples
0	$11,420	$18,440
5,000	$8,920	$15,940
10,000	$6,420	$13,440
15,000	$5,160	$10,940
20,000	$5,160	$10,320
25,000	$5,160	$10,320
30,000	$4,350	$9,510
35,000	$3,350	$8,510
40,000	$2,350	$7,510
45,000	$1,350	$6,510
50,000	$350	$5,510
60,000	0	$3,510
70,000	0	$1,510
80,000	0	0

[1] Includes income from Canada/Quebec Pension Plans, but excludes income from OAS/GIS, which the Seniors Benefit would replace.

Source: *The Seniors Benefit - Securing the Future* (Ottawa: Government of Canada, March 1996, p. 30).

Senior citizens with no income from other sources would be eligible for the maximum benefit. As outlined in the 1996 federal budget, the maximum benefit in the year 2001 would be $951 a month or $11,420 a year for singles, and $1537 a month or $18,440 a year for couples. These amounts are equal to the 1997 combined maximum of OAS/GIS benefits plus an additional $10 a month or $120 a year. Recipients of the Spouse's Allowance would also receive an additional $10 a month under the changes proposed in 1996. The Seniors Benefit would be reduced as family income from other sources rose, and it would disappear when such income reached about $52,000 for singles and $78,000 for couples (see Table 12).

Compared to the old age benefits system as it stood in 1997, the proposed Seniors Benefit would be targeted more to individuals and couples with low incomes, and it would reduce benefits for high-income senior citizens. According to estimates by the federal Department of Finance, single senior citizens and couples with annual incomes of less than about $40,000 would receive the same benefits, or better, under the proposed changes. Once a couple's annual income reached $45,000, their benefits would begin to drop, falling to zero at an annual income of $78,000. All single people with annual incomes above $40,000 would receive less as a result of the proposed changes than they get under the present system. Their benefits would gradually be reduced to zero as their annual incomes rose to $52,000.

The Canada and Quebec Pension Plans

Background

The introduction of the Canada Pension Plan (CPP) in 1966 was the result of intense federal and provincial negotiations in the early part of the decade.[32] Initially, the provinces were not enthusiastic about the idea of a new national contributory pension plan, but a federal offer of low-cost loans through the CPP fund and a provision to have provincial rights written into the CPP Act, persuaded the provinces to participate. Quebec agreed to the concept following a federal offer to allow the provinces to opt out of the national scheme if they set up a parallel plan of their own. Quebec was the only province to take up this offer, establishing the Quebec Pension Plan (QPP) in 1966.[33]

Benefits under the Canada and Quebec Pension Plans (CPP/QPP) were phased in between 1967 and 1976, when virtually all Canadians in the labour force became members of one of the two plans. CPP/QPP retirement benefits were designed to replace about one-quarter of a contributor's earnings (up to a "maximum pensionable earnings") averaged over the course of their working life.[34] The plans also provided contributors with survivor and disability insurance benefits.

During the 1970s, public pressure led to improvements in women's coverage under the Canada and Quebec Pension Plans. Survivor benefits were equalized for men and women, and a new provision was instituted to split the value of cumulative CPP/QPP contributions or credits equally between spouses at the dissolution of a marriage. Another change aimed at improving women's CPP/QPP benefit levels occurred in the late 1970s, when most of the provinces and the federal government agreed to omit from the calculation of retirement benefits women's years of low earnings due to child rearing. However, stalling by Ontario using its veto power held up this change until the early 1980s.

In the 1980s, concerns grew that contributions to the CPP/QPP would not be sufficient to support the surge of baby-boomers retiring, beginning in the year 2011. Experts argued that contribution increases, if made well in advance of this demographic shift, would minimize the financial pressures on the plans in later years. Although this was a long-standing concern, it was not until 1985 that governments approved contribution rate increases, the first of which came two years later.[35]

A 1985 federal-provincial agreement established a schedule of gradual annual rate increases for CPP contributions. The QPP responded with a similar schedule of rate increases. The federal and provincial governments also agreed to publish a 25-year schedule of projected CPP contribution rates based on estimates of future demands on the fund. In addition, they agreed to meet every five years to review these projections and make any necessary adjustments. Following suit, Quebec established its own review schedule. The first national review took place in 1991.

The Current Canada and Quebec Pension Plans

The Canada and Quebec Pension Plans are contributory, earnings-related, social insurance programs that provide benefits in the case of retirement, death, and disability.[36] The CPP and QPP are jointly financed by employees and employers; virtually all Canadians in the workforce contribute to one plan or the other.[37]

The CPP is administered by Human Resources Development Canada, and contributions to the plan are collected by Revenue Canada. The Quebec Ministry of Revenue collects contributions for the QPP, while the Régie des rentes du Quebec administers the plan's benefits. Although the two plans are run separately, they are fully coordinated – notwithstanding some minor differences between the two – and contributions are portable between the two plans.

The broad policy directions of the CPP are set and reviewed jointly by the federal and provincial governments. All changes to the CPP require the consent of two-thirds of the provinces representing two-thirds of the population. Ongoing collaboration between administrators of the Canada and Quebec Pension Plans has resulted in a great deal of consistency between the plans. The most recent federal-provincial review of the CPP took place in 1996 and lead to a series of reforms which took effect on January 1, 1998.[38] In June 1997, the Quebec government announced that it would adopt many of the changes approved for the CPP.[39]

Contributions
In 1997, persons between the ages of 18 and 65 were required to make CPP/QPP contributions on earnings between $3,500 (the Yearly Basic Exemption or YBE) and $35,800 (the Yearly Maximum Pensionable Earnings or YMPE).[40] The combined employer-employee CPP contribution rate that year was 5.85

per cent of pensionable earnings, that is, earnings between the YBE and the YMPE.

Under the 1997 federal-provincial agreement, the combined CPP employer-employee contribution rate rose to six per cent for 1997.[41] This brought the CPP rate into line with the 1997 QPP employer-employee rate. While employees are responsible for only half of the combined employer-employee rate, self-employed persons pay the full rate based on the pensionable earnings component of their net business income.

Following the rate change, the maximum annual CPP/QPP *employee* contribution rose to $969 in 1997; the maximum contribution for self-employed persons was $1,938. These amounts were reduced – by approximately $262 for employees and $523 for the self-employed – through federal and provincial tax credits when contributors filed their 1997 tax returns.[42]

Nearly 10 million Canadians contributed $10.6 billion to the Canada Pension Plan in 1996. Another 3.1 million Quebecers contributed $3.2 billion to the Quebec Pension Plan that year.[43]

Changes to CPP/QPP Contributions

In addition to increasing the CPP contribution rate that year, the 1997 federal-provincial agreement established a new 25-year contribution rate schedule (see Table 13 below). On the old schedule, the combined employee-employer rate was to rise gradually to approximately 14 per cent of pensionable earnings by 2030, by which time the majority of the baby-boomers would have reached retirement age. Under the new schedule, the rate will rise to a maximum of 9.9 per cent of pensionable earnings – referred to as the "steady-state" rate – but the increase will be phased in by 2003, much more quickly than under the old plan. In June 1997, the Quebec government announced that the QPP would adopt this new CPP rate schedule.

Until 1997, the CPP contribution schedule was reviewed once every five years by the federal and provincial governments. The 1997 federal-provincial agreement changed this review process to once every three years in order to improve the response time to changes in economic circumstances. The new agreement also gives the CPP's Chief Actuary the authority to make adjustments to the contribution schedule between federal-provincial meetings, if necessary. The government of Quebec also plans to review the QPP schedule every three years.

Table 13

CPP Contribution Rate Schedule		
Year	Schedule before 1997 Reforms Combined employee-employer rate (%)	New Schedule Combined employee-employer rate (%)
1997	5.85	6.0
1998	6.10	6.4
1999	6.35	7.0
2000	6.60	7.8
2001	6.85	8.6
2002	7.10	9.4
2003	7.35	9.9
2004	7.60	9.9
2005	7.85	9.9
2016	10.10	9.9
2030	14.20	9.9
Source: *Securing the Canada Pension Plan* (Ottawa: Human Resources Development Canada, February 1997, p. 11).		

In addition to increasing the CPP contribution rate and establishing more frequent monitoring procedures of rate changes required, the 1997 agreement also increased the size of the CPP fund by expanding the base upon which contributions are paid. The CPP's Yearly Basic Exemption (YBE) was frozen, meaning that it would no longer increase with inflation. Quebec announced that it would introduce the same measure for the QPP. By freezing the YBE, the yearly pensionable earnings of all CPP/QPP contributors will rise, in real terms, over time, thus expanding the base upon which contributions are calculated.

Funding

The Canada and Quebec Pension Plans operate on a "pay-as-you-go" basis: current contributors pay into the plans to support current beneficiaries. CPP contributions that are not required to pay for current benefits or administration are placed in a CPP reserve fund. The CPP reserve fund generally holds about two years' worth of benefits. Traditionally, these funds were loaned to the provinces at the 20-year federal bond rate. By contrast, the QPP has a longstanding arrangement with the Caisse de dépôt et placement du Québec to invest monies raised through QPP contributions in a diversified portfolio.

As part of the 1997 federal-provincial agreement, the Canada Pension Plan will end its practice of lending CPP reserve funds to the provinces. Instead, it will invest these funds in a diversified portfolio, as does Quebec. This measure, along with the higher contribution rate, the larger contribution base, and other changes aimed at reducing the amount of money spent on CPP benefits, is expected to increase the size of the CPP reserve fund from two to five years' worth of benefits. This will provide a larger financial cushion to accommodate future demands on the fund as baby-boomers reach retirement age.

Retirement Benefits

Anyone who has contributed to the Canada or Quebec Pension Plans is eligible for a retirement pension after their 60th birthday. However, the size of the pension benefit varies according to the following factors: an individual's earnings; his or her age; and, his or her CPP/QPP contributions while in the labour force. CPP/QPP contributors can request a Statement of Contributions[44] to determine what their retirement benefits would be if they were to retire at that moment. The 1997 federal-provincial agreement announced that these statements would be provided annually to CPP contributors "as soon as is feasible."[45]

The maximum monthly CPP/QPP retirement benefit is available to contributors at age 65. In 1997, it was equal to 25 per cent of one-twelfth of the average Yearly Maximum Pensionable Earnings (YMPE) during the three years prior to filing a claim (i.e., the year that one applies for benefits, plus the two preceding years). The maximum CPP/QPP retirement benefit in 1997 was $737 per month or $8,842 per year. The method of calculating the YMPE changed in 1998, to include the four most recent years of earnings; in 1999, it will be calculated on the five most recent years of earnings. As a result of these changes, the federal government estimates that the maximum CPP/QPP retirement benefit will fall slightly to $724 per month or $8,688 per year (in 1997 dollars) by 1999, thereby reducing expenditures for CPP/QPP benefits from the fund.

Although Canada and Quebec Pension Plan contributors can begin to collect retirement benefits when they turn 60, they can also wait as late as age 70 to begin collecting their benefits. The amount received is adjusted actuarially to recognize that those who receive benefits at an earlier age will be collecting for a longer time period than those who retire later. For early retirees, benefits are *reduced* by half a per cent for each month between the first CPP/QPP cheque and the recipient's 65th birthday. The maximum reduction is 30 per cent. For those who do not receive any CPP payments until after their 65th birthday, the benefits are *increased* by half a per cent for each month between the first month after their 65th birthday and the month in which the first payment is made. The maximum increase in benefits is 30 per cent, for those who wait until age 70. Other than inflation adjustments, the monthly CPP/QPP benefit does not change throughout the recipient's retirement.

The Canada and Quebec Pension Plans have a number of provisions that protect beneficiaries against periods of low earnings during their working life . A standard "drop-out" clause allows all contributors to exclude up to 15 per cent of their contributory period from the calculation of their CPP/QPP benefit. This provision is designed primarily to assist those who experience periods of low (or no) earnings due to illness, unemployment, education, or retraining. Contributors can also exclude periods of low or no earnings as a result of caring for a child under the age of seven. In addition, any time spent by a contributor on CPP disability benefits is also excluded from the retirement benefit calculation.

Those who continue to work and make CPP contributions beyond age 65 have an opportunity to make up for low earnings during their normal contributory period (ages 18 to 65 years). Individuals can use each month of pensionable earnings after age 65 to replace previous months of low earnings. Until 1997, participants in the Quebec plan over age 65 were not required to make QPP contributions, nor were their employers. Beginning in 1998, however, these individuals and their employers will contribute to the plan, but they will not have the option of "making up" for past years of low contributions.

Canada and Quebec Pension Plan retirement benefits are paid to eligible persons in Canada and abroad. Under the CPP, upon application by either spouse, married or common-law couples can share all or a portion of their retirement benefits, depending on how long they have been together. Quebec recently recognized this right as well. While contributing to the Canada and Quebec Pension Plans, individuals accumulate credits. Under the CPP, these credits *must* be split upon the dissolution of marriage or common-law relationship; under the QPP, credits *can* be split between the partners upon divorce, but this does not apply to common-law couples. The credits entitle individuals to a variety of CPP/QPP benefits.

Canada and Quebec Pension Plan retirement benefits are taxable and fully indexed to inflation. In 1996, an average of 2.4 million Canadians received CPP retirement benefits each month, at a cost of $11 billion that year.[46] Another 806,000 people received QPP retirement benefits each month in 1996, totalling about $3.4 billion.[47]

Disability Benefits

In addition to retirement benefits, the Canada and Quebec
Pension Plans also provide contributors with support if they are
unable to work due to a disability.[48] In order to qualify for CPP
or QPP disability benefits, individuals must be "unable to work
due to a severe and prolonged disability." The QPP has different
provisions for people between the ages of 60 and 65; these
individuals are eligible if they can no longer do their job due to
health reasons.

CPP disability claimants must be between the ages of 18 and 65,
and they must have contributed to the plan for at least two of
the three years, or five of the 10 years, prior to making a claim.
These requirements also apply to the QPP. The QPP also
extends eligibility to those who have made contributions during
at least half of their contributory period (a minimum of two
years).

The CPP/QPP disability benefit consists of a flat-rate portion that
is unrelated to previous earnings, plus an earnings-related
component. The earnings-related component is equal to 75 per
cent of a CPP/QPP retirement pension, calculated as if the
applicant were retiring at age 65 at the time of their disability
benefit application. Applicants must wait for three months after
the disability has occurred before they can receive benefits.

In 1997, the maximum monthly CPP/QPP disability benefit was
$883 or $10,597 a year. Benefits generally start about four
months after an application is accepted. Payments stop if any of
the following situations occur: the individual no longer meets
the definition of "disability" under the CPP/QPP Act; the
recipient begins collecting CPP/QPP retirement benefits; or, the
recipient dies.

Canada Pension Plan officials check periodically to ensure that
beneficiaries still meet the definition of disability under the Act.
CPP disability recipients may perform volunteer work or attend
school and still be eligible for benefits, as long as their disability

continues to prohibit them from working. Some disability benefit recipients may also receive vocational rehabilitation services designed to reintegrate them into the workforce. Benefits continue to be paid for three months after the individual resumes working. If the disability reoccurs and again prevents the individual from working, their reapplication for benefits is fast-tracked.

Canada and Quebec Pension Plan disability recipients with dependants under the age of 18 years – or in the case of the CPP, between ages 18 and 25, if the dependants are still in school – are eligible for a supplemental child's benefit.[49] The child's benefit is set at a flat rate. In 1997, the rate was $167 per month (or $2,000 a year) under the CPP, and $53 per month (or $635 a year) for the QPP. While the Canada Pension Plan provides a child benefit to each claimant in families where both parents receive disability insurance, the Quebec Pension Plan pays only one benefit. Under both plans, the child's benefit stops if the parent is no longer eligible for disability benefits, if the child no longer meets the age requirements, or if the child dies. The CPP/QPP child's benefit is fully indexed to inflation.

As part of the 1997 federal-provincial agreement, the administration of CPP disability benefits is to be tightened due to a rapid escalation in the costs of the program, particularly in comparison to those in the Quebec plan. One major change requires individuals to have contributed to the CPP (on earnings of at least $3,500 a year – the YBE) for at least four of the last six years, rather than for two of the last three years, or five of the last 10 years, as was required before the 1997 agreement. The Quebec Pension Plan continues to operate its own disability eligibility rules which are generally applied more stringently than the CPP rules.

The 1997 agreement also introduced a new method of calculating benefits for those individuals who move directly from CPP disability benefits to CPP retirement benefits upon reaching age 65 years. As of 1998, the calculation of retirement benefits is based on the YMPE at the time of the disability, with subsequent indexing for full inflation, rather than on the YMPE at the time the individual reaches retirement age. No previous disability beneficiaries will be affected by these changes. Similarly, in 1998, the Quebec Pension Plan is replacing the full retirement pension available to disability recipients at age 65 years with an actuarially adjusted pension that reflects the time that an individual collected QPP disability benefits between the ages of 60 and 65.

As part of the 1997 federal-provincial CPP agreement, it was announced that disability benefits would no longer be paid to estates, and persons already receiving early CPP retirement benefits would no longer be eligible for disability benefits. By contrast, the QPP continues to pay disability benefits to estates and allows plan members to apply for disability benefits up to 18 months after they have started collecting early retirement benefits, a change from the previous six-month limit.

In 1996, an average of 299,000 Canadians received CPP disability benefits each month, at a cost of $2.5 billion. Of this group, 104,000 people – or about one-third of all disability benefit recipients – also received the child's benefit, at an additional cost of $251 million.[50] Another 48,000 people received QPP disability benefits that year, costing $431 million. About 9,000 people in this group also received the child benefit, at a cost of $7 million.[51]

Survivor and Death Benefits
The Canada and Quebec Pension Plans offer several types of payments to relatives in the event of the contributor's death. These include a surviving spouse's pension, a lump-sum death benefit, and an orphan's benefit.

The eligibility requirements for a surviving spouse's pension vary according to the length of the deceased's contributory period. In cases where the contributory period was less than nine years, the deceased must have contributed to the CPP/QPP for at least three years. If their contributory period was longer than nine years, the deceased must have contributed to CPP/QPP for at least one-third of their contributory period, or 10 years, whichever is less. (If the contributor died before the age of 65, the contributory period ends in the month in which the death occurred). The Canada Pension Plan also requires that the surviving spouse be at least 35 years of age, unless they have a disability or care for dependent children. This requirement does not apply in the Quebec plan.

There are two basic categories of survivor benefit recipients in the Canada and Quebec Pension Plans: those over age 65 and those under age 65. Surviving spouses aged 65 and older receive a pension equal to 60 per cent of the retirement pension that the deceased contributor would have received at age 65. Surviving spouses under the age of 65 receive a pension that is composed of two parts: a flat-rate portion and an earnings-related portion. The CPP and the QPP differ in the method of calculating the flat-rate portion for recipients under the age of 65 years.

Under both the Canada and Quebec Pension Plans, all survivors under age 65 years receive an earnings-related benefit equal to 37.5 per cent of the actual or calculated retirement pension of the deceased contributor. The CPP adds a single flat-rate portion to this amount for all eligible recipients (although survivors' pensions are reduced for younger recipients, see below). By contrast, the QPP pays a flat-rate portion that varies, depending on the age of the recipient and whether or not they have dependent children or a disability.

Under both the Canada and Quebec Pension Plans, the maximum that survivors over the age of 65 could receive in 1997 was $442 per month or $5,305 a year. The maximum Canada Pension Plan survivor's benefit for those under age 65 was $405 a month or $4,863 a year in 1997. This maximum is composed of a $129 flat-rate portion plus an earnings-related portion of up to $276, for a total of $405 a month. Surviving spouses between

35 and 45 years old who have no dependent children nor a disability have their pension reduced by one-twelfth for each month that their age is less than 45 years at the time of the contributor's death.

Under the Quebec Pension Plan, the maximum earnings-related portion of a survivor's pension in 1997 was $276 per month (or $3,316 per year) for all recipients, regardless of their age. In addition to this amount, survivors under the age of 45 were eligible for a flat-rate benefit calculated in the following way: $85 per month (or $1,016 per year) if they had neither a disability nor dependent children; $307 per month (or $3,682 per year) if they were able-bodied with dependent children; and $330 per month (or $3,966 per year) if they had a disability. Survivors aged 45 to 54 were eligible for a flat-rate benefit of up to $330 per month (or $3,966 per year), while those aged 55 to 64 received a flat-rate benefit of $400 per month (or $4,795 per year).

In 1996, an average of 763,000 Canadians received surviving spouse's benefits each month, at a cost of $2.3 billion for the year.[52] Another 273,000 people received survivor benefits under the QPP, totalling one billion dollars that year.[53]

Some surviving spouses with dependants or other guardians of the deceased's dependants are also eligible for an orphan's benefit under both the Canada and Quebec Pension Plans. Age requirements for this benefit mirror those of the child's benefit for persons receiving CPP/QPP disability benefits. The maximum CPP orphan's benefit in 1997 was $167 per month (or $2,000 a year), while the QPP paid a monthly maximum of $53 or $635 a year. In 1996, an average of 90,000 CPP survivor benefit recipients also received the orphan's benefit each month, at a cost of $198 million that year.[54] Another 30,000 survivor benefit recipients under the QPP received the orphan's benefit, at a cost of $20 million for the year.[55]

Upon the death of a CPP or QPP contributor, a lump-sum death benefit is paid to the estate, as long as contributions had been made to the plan for the minimum qualifying period (the same minimum as for the surviving spouse's pension). The death benefit is paid whether a will or estate exists or not. It is equal to six times the monthly retirement pension of the deceased contributor, or roughly 10 per cent of the YMPE, whichever is less. In 1997, this amounted to a maximum death benefit of $3,580. In 1996, the CPP fund paid out $241 million in death benefits,[56] and the QPP paid out $80 million.[57]

Under the 1997 federal-provincial agreement, governments agreed to continue calculating the death benefit as equivalent to six months' worth of retirement benefits, but the benefit limit was lowered to $2,500 and was no longer indexed to inflation. That year, the Quebec government announced that it would provide a flat-rate death benefit of $2,500.

Combined Benefits

In cases where an individual is eligible for more than one benefit under either the Canada or Quebec Pension Plan, a combined benefit is paid, subject to specific maximums.

Under both the CPP and the QPP, the maximum combined retirement/survivor benefit is equivalent to the maximum retirement benefit. The method of calculating the combined survivor/disability benefit is more complicated. Under the CPP, the survivor/disability benefit is the greater of the two flat-rate components, plus the lesser of the two earnings-related components, up to the equivalent of the maximum retirement pension payable during the year in which the beneficiary becomes eligible for the second benefit. By contrast, the QPP combined survivor/disability benefit is equal to the total of the two benefits, less the flat-rate portion of the disability benefit.

The 1997 federal-provincial agreement announced changes to the method of calculating CPP combined benefits. Starting in 1998, someone who is aged 65 or older and eligible for both the survivor's benefit and the retirement benefit receives the higher of the two benefits, plus 60 per cent of the lower benefit. The maximum has remained unchanged. Those eligible for both a survivor's benefit and a disability benefit receive the larger of the two flat-rate portions plus the larger of the earnings-related portions, as well as 60 per cent of the smaller of the earnings-related portions. This combination must not exceed the maximum disability benefit. The rules governing combined benefit maximums have remained unchanged under the Quebec Pension Plan.

In 1997, the maximum combined survivor/retirement benefit (for those up to age 65) under both the Canada and Quebec Pension Plans was $737 per month or $8,842 per year. The maximum CPP benefit for individuals eligible for both the survivor's and disability benefits was $1,067 per month or $12,808 per year. This maximum also applied to individuals under the age of 55 in the Quebec plan. Under the QPP, people between the ages of 55 and 65 received up to $1,136 per month (or $13,632 per year) in 1997. In 1996, an average of 371,000 Canadians received combined benefits under CPP each month.[58] Another 110,000 people received QPP combined benefits each month in 1996.[59]

Private Pension and Retirement Savings Plans

Background

Private pension plans in Canada originated in the 1800s, and the legal and regulatory structures for private retirement savings plans were first developed during the early 1900s.[60] Substantial changes to these legal and regulatory structures were made by governments in the 1950s. Today, private pension plans and retirement savings plans are key components of the retirement income security system in Canada. They are supported by a combination of government regulations and tax supports.

Pension plans in Canada followed on the heels of rapid industrialization in the mid-1800s. The first workers' pension plan was developed for federal public service employees in 1870. In 1874, the Grand Trunk Railway became Canada's first private sector company to set up a pension plan for its workers. These milestones were followed by the Government Annuities Act in 1908 which allowed individuals to save for their retirement by purchasing government annuities. Several years later, the addition of group contracts under this program contributed to a growth in the number of workplace pension plans. Federal tax changes over the next decade made employer and employee contributions to these plans tax exempt and helped encourage the establishment of pension plans. In the 1930s, limits to these tax breaks were set.

The number of pension plans in Canada expanded rapidly during the 1940s and the immediate postwar period. Labour unions, particularly in the growing automotive industry, pushed employers to provide pensions as a form of deferred wages and a way of avoiding wartime wage and price controls. Many other large unions soon followed suit, prompting employers in non-unionized settings to establish pensions which became a major issue of the time.[61]

In 1957, the Income Tax Act was amended to provide individuals who were not covered by pension plans – including the self-employed – with similar tax advantages to those enjoyed by pension plan members. These changes allowed individuals to deduct contributions to a Registered Retirement Savings Plan (RRSP), up to a certain limit, from their taxable income. Tax that would normally be paid was deferred until the money was withdrawn from the RRSP, usually at retirement. In 1961, similar provisions were made for employer-established deferred profit-sharing programs. The original private savings plan

provided under the Government Annuities Act was disbanded in
1975.

Between the mid-1960s and mid-1980s, the federal and
provincial governments implemented legislation to more tightly
govern the operation of pension plans. This came about in
response to concerns about wide variations in the ways that
pension plans were administered and concerns about the
portability of the plans and the provision of survivor benefits.
During the 1980s and early 1990s, federal-provincial negotiations resulted in legislative changes in most jurisdictions
designed to establish minimum standards for pension plans
across the country.

During this time, the federal government also increased the
allowable contribution limits for RRSPs and workplace pension
plans (now referred to as Registered Pension Plans or RPPs) in
order to encourage increased individual savings for retirement.[62] However, the schedule for new contribution limits was
scaled back in the mid-1990s amid concerns about the rising
cost to the federal government of providing such tax subsidies.[63]

The Current Private Pension
and Retirement System

In addition to the old age security system and the Canada and
Quebec Pension Plans, many Canadians contribute to and
benefit from private retirement pension plans such as employer-
sponsored plans – also known as Registered Pension Plans
(RPPs) – and private savings programs such as Registered
Retirement Savings Plans (RRSPs). Some individuals also benefit
from deferred profit-sharing programs (DPSPs) sponsored by
their employers to supplement retirement incomes. Although
privately administered,[64] these plans are subject to federal and
provincial legislation. Individuals also receive government

support to invest in these plans through incentives built into the income tax system.

Registered Pension Plans

Registered Pension Plans are employee retirement benefit programs established by individual employers, groups of employers, or unions.[65] They are found in both the public and private sectors. All levels of government, including government agencies, provide public sector pension plans.

Regulatory authority for RPPs is shared between the federal and provincial governments. The federal government administers the Pension Benefit Standards Act which covers federally regulated industries such as banking and telecommunications. Provincial governments are responsible for workers in all industries under provincial jurisdiction.

There are several types of RPPs including both contributory and non-contributory plans. In contributory plans, employers (including unions and employer groups) and their employees share the costs of the plan through payroll deductions generally ranging from five to ten per cent of earnings. Non-contributory plans are funded entirely by employers. Employee and employer contributions to RPPs are tax deductible within established limits. About three-quarters of RPP members belong to contributory plans; the remaining one-quarter belong to non-contributory plans.

Registered Pension Plans can also be either a "defined benefit" or "defined contribution" plan. Defined benefit plans guarantee contributors a fixed percentage of their earnings upon retirement for each year of employment. One commonly used formula takes the average of an employee's five best years of earnings and provides two per cent of this amount for each year of their service. Ninety per cent of Canadians who belong to an RPP are part of a defined benefit plan. Most of the remainder belong to defined contribution plans.

Members of a defined contribution or "money purchase" plan are assigned their own pension account which accumulates assets through contributions – made by themselves and their employers – plus compounding returns on investments.

Neither the accumulated contributions nor interest income in an RPP are taxable while they remain in the account. However, employee contributions are tax deductible up to a limit of $13,500 per year or 18 per cent of income, whichever is less, and contributors must limit the foreign content of their total RPP portfolio to no more than 20 per cent.[66]

Upon retirement, money accumulated in an account is generally converted into an "annuity" which pays the recipient a fixed amount, usually on a monthly basis. Once money is removed from the registered retirement account, it is then taxable. Since annuities are not usually indexed to inflation, members of defined contribution plans are not protected against the erosive effects of inflation on their retirement income over time.

Just under half of all Canadians in the paid labour force are members of a Registered Pension Plan. The public sector provides the best coverage for its employees: 85 per cent of public sector workers are covered by RPPs, compared to about 33 per cent of workers in the private sector. As well, many public sector pension plans provide retirement benefits that are indexed to inflation, while most private sector plans do not provide such protection.

In the private sector, members of RPPs are most likely to work in large businesses and in male-dominated and unionized industries. About two-thirds of RPP members work in firms with 1,000 or more employees. And more than twice as many men as women are members of these plans.

Middle- and high-income earners are more likely to belong to a Registered Pension Plan than low-income earners. Over half of all Canadian employees with annual incomes above $40,000 per year belong to an RPP. By contrast, only one-third of employees with annual incomes between $20,000 and $30,000 belong to such a plan, and less than one-tenth of those with incomes below $20,000 are members of an RPP. Tax benefits for contributions to an RPP also rise with income levels: the higher one's income, the larger the tax break for pension plan contributions.

In 1996, 5.1 million Canadians contributed $19.7 billion to Registered Pension Plans.[67] As a result, the federal government lost about $16.5 billion that year in foregone tax revenues on contributions to RPPs and interest earned on the sheltered income. Approximately $5 billion was recovered in taxes charged on money withdrawn from RPPs, resulting in a net cost to the federal government of about $11.5 billion that year. The net cost to provincial governments in foregone tax revenues for RPPs that year was approximately $6.5 billion.[68]

Although the specific regulations that guide the administration of RPPs vary from one province to the next, a 1986 federal-provincial agreement improved the standards and uniformity of regulations across the country. Today, RPPs in Canada are required to meet basic standards with regard to plan membership, the "vesting" or "locking-in" of benefits, the portability of pensions, and the provision of benefits to survivors. For example, all federally regulated industries and most provincially regulated industries must allow full-time employees to become members of an existing Registered Pension Plan after two years employment with a given employer. Part-time workers must be allowed to join an RPP if they earn at least 35 per cent of the CPP/QPP Yearly Maximum Pensionable Earnings for two consecutive years. Employers have the option of making membership in their pension plan either voluntary or automatic.

Federal and provincial governments also regulate the vesting of pensions which requires that employees who change jobs be entitled to receive their accumulated contributions – both the contributions they made, as well as those made by their employer on their behalf – under defined contribution plans, or their benefits earned to date in the case of defined benefit plans. When workers change jobs, they receive their pension benefits, but they are required to lock them in until retirement age, generally not before age 55. This ensures that money intended to support an individual in their retirement is not spent immediately.

Changes in RPP regulations over the years have also improved the portability of pension plan benefits, although full portability does not yet exist. Today, most members of these plans can transfer their benefits to a new employer's pension plan when they change jobs, or the benefits can be transferred to an individual RRSP account or to an annuity where the monies are locked in until retirement.

The federal and provincial governments have also agreed that all Registered Pension Plans must provide survivor benefits to spouses of deceased plan members. The plans must provide a survivor benefit of at least 60 per cent of the pension that would have been received by the deceased plan member.[69] The surviving spouse continues to receive these benefits even if they remarry. In cases where a plan member dies before retirement, most jurisdictions require that all or part of the vested benefits be transferred to the surviving spouse, either as a lump-sum cash payment or as a transfer to an RRSP or annuity.

Registered Retirement Savings Plans
Registered Retirement Savings Plans (RRSPs) are designed to encourage Canadians to save privately for their retirement.[70] Since contributions to an RRSP and returns on investments within an RRSP are *not* subject to income tax, individuals are able to accumulate substantial savings for their retirement through this vehicle. Taxes are paid only when money is removed from the RRSP. These and other RRSP rules are set out in the Income Tax Act which is monitored and enforced by Revenue Canada.

Individuals who do not belong to either a Registered Pension Plan or a Deferred Profit Sharing Plan are allowed to contribute up to 18 per cent of their previous year's earnings to a Registered Retirement Savings Plan, to a maximum of $13,500 per year, including contributions made by employers on the employee's behalf.[71] This limit is decreased by any amount contributed to a spouse's RRSP, or by any amount contributed to an RPP or DPSP throughout the year, or the value of pension credits earned. This is referred to as a Pension Adjustment (PA).[72] An individual can increase their contributions beyond the standard annual limit by carrying forward any unused "RRSP room" from previous years. This provision enables individuals to maximize their RRSP contribu-tions over several years and to compensate for years in which they did not make their full, allowable RRSP contribution.[73]

Individuals interested in establishing an RRSP can do so at authorized financial institutions such as banks, trust companies, or credit unions.[74] These institutions receive permission from Revenue Canada to set up personalized RRSP accounts, and they are well-versed in the relevant RRSP rules and regulations.

RRSP contributors can choose from a range of investment vehicles – such as Guaranteed Investment Certificates (GICs) and mutual funds – offered by their financial institution. In most cases, contribu-tors can also choose to "self-direct" their RRSP, which allows them to select investment vehicles (such as GICs, stocks, bonds, or mutual funds) beyond those offered by the institution where they have established their

Calculating one's RRSP contribution limit

Andrée earned $40,000 in the 1996 taxation year. Her RRSP limit for 1997 was $7,200 (18 per cent of her 1996 earnings), less her Pension Adjustment, plus any unused RRSP room from previous years. Assuming that she contributed $4,200 to an RPP in 1996 and had $5,000 of unused RRSP room, she would have a 1997 RRSP limit of $8,000: $7,200 + $5,000 minus $4,200. Andrée's 1997 RRSP limit would be indicated on the 1996 Notice of Assessment or Reassessment she received from Revenue Canada.

RRSP. In either case, contributors must limit the foreign content of their RRSP portfolio to no more than 20 per cent of the total value.

As of 1997, RRSP contributors are required to withdraw all of their RRSP savings in the year they turn 69 years old, or they must convert their RRSP into a Registered Retirement Income Fund (RRIF) or some other retirement income option. (Before 1997, contributors had until age 71 to do so.)[75] Most individuals convert their RRSP savings into an annuity that pays them fixed monthly amounts, or to a Registered Retirement Income Fund (RRIF) which provides them with benefits that increase over time. The incremental increase in payments under the RRIF provides a form of protection against inflation. For those who convert their RRSP into either an annuity or RRIF, only the monthly dispersements – and not the total accumulated savings – are subject to tax.

In 1996, 6 million Canadians – more than one-third of all Canadian tax filers – held an RRSP. Total RRSP contributions that year were $26.2 billion, compared to $12.3 billion in 1991.[76] The cost to the federal government in foregone taxes on RRSP contributions and lost revenues on the earned investment income was about $10.5 billion, compared to $4 billion in 1991. Approximately $2 billion was recovered through federal taxes collected on monies withdrawn from RRSPs, resulting in a net cost to the federal government of about $8.5 billion for the 1996 taxation year. The net cost to the provinces that year was approximately $4.5 billion.[77]

High-income earners contribute the most to RRSPs, on average.[78] Because these individuals generally fall into the higher tax brackets, they also receive the largest tax breaks for their contributions. However, even the highest-income earners use only about one-half of their available RRSP room. Unused RRSP room in 1997 totalled $216 billion, up from just $45 billion in 1991.[79]

In 1996, 851,000 Canadians removed $4.4 billion from their RRSPs. This represents eighty-five cents removed for every five dollars put into an RRSP. [80]

Deferred Profit Sharing Plans

Deferred Profit Sharing Plans (DPSPs) are savings vehicles used by employers to distribute corporate profits to their employees.[81] Through a DPSP program, employers are entitled to make tax-free contributions, up to an established limit, to individual savings accounts on behalf of their employees. Although DPSPs are not necessarily designated as retirement savings plans, they generally serve that purpose.

Like RRSPs, guidelines which govern the use of DPSPs are found in the Income Tax Act. These guidelines are administered by the federal government through Revenue Canada. Among other things, the guidelines establish the annual limit for tax-free DPSP contributions. In 1997, the limit was set at one-half of the maximum RPP/RRSP contribution limit – an amount equal to $6,750.[82]

The Income Tax Act also specifies the responsibilities of employers who operate DPSPs, the rules regarding transfers between DPSPs, RRSPs and RPPs, and the tax treatment of benefits removed from a DPSP. For example, if an employee leaves their job, they have the option of transferring their accumulated DPSP benefits to an RPP or RRSP. As well, contributors can convert their DPSP benefits into an annuity or RRIF (usually at retirement), or they can choose a lump-sum payment. As with RRSPs, lump-sum payments are immediately taxable, while only the monthly installments of an annuity or RRIF are subject to tax.

Endnotes

1. Unless otherwise indicated, the information for this section was taken from Dennis Guest, *The Emergence of Social Security in Canada* (Vancouver: University of British Columbia Press, 1985), and from *Canada's Retirement Income Programs: A Statistical Overview* (Ottawa: Statistics Canada, 1996).

2. Michael Prince, "Lowering the Boom on the Boomers: Replacing Old Age Security with the New Seniors Benefit and Reforming the Canada Pension Plan," in *How Ottawa Spends – 1997-98* (Ottawa: Carleton University Press, 1997, p. 214).

3. Ken Battle, "A New Old Age Pension," in *Conference on the Retirement Income System* (Kingston, Ontario: School of Policy Studies, Queen's University, February 1996).

4. *Canada's Retirement Income Programs: A Statistical Overview* (Ottawa: Statistics Canada, 1996, p. 34).

5. *Annual Statistics on the Canada Pension Plan and Old Age Security* (Ottawa: Human Resources Development Canada, 1997, p. 187).

6. Unless otherwise indicated, information for this section was taken from *Overview: Income Security Programs – Old Age Security, Canada Pension Plan* (Ottawa: Human Resources Development Canada, 1994), and from *Your Old Age Security Pension* (Ottawa: Human Resources Development Canada, 1996). The monthly benefit rates are for October to December 1997, as identified in *ISP - Information Card* (Ottawa: Human Resources Development Canada, 1997). Benefit amounts have been rounded to the nearest dollar.

7. It *is* possible to qualify for an OAS pension without residing in Canada for a total of 40 years. For example, most people residing in Canada prior to 1997 have the option of applying for OAS under the "old" residence rules, which permitted a qualifying period of 10 years of residence prior to pension approval. As well, persons with absences within this 10-year period may compensate with periods of prior presence in Canada, as long as the previous periods were three times the length of the absence, and as long as there was a final full year of Canadian residence prior to benefit approval.

8. *Budget Plan* (Ottawa: Government of Canada, 1996, p. 66).

9. OAS payments are made indefinitely for recipients with 20 years or more of residency in Canada, regardless of where the individual chooses to live. By

contrast, payments are stopped for those with less than 20 years residency in Canada if the applicant leaves the country for more than six months.

10. *Budget Plan* (Ottawa: Government of Canada, 1995, p. 58).

11. "Income" refers to "net income" as used for tax purposes. Net income includes earnings, interest and other income, less deductions such as RRSP contributions. This definition is used throughout this chapter.

12. *Annual Statistics on the Canada Pension Plan and Old Age Security* (Ottawa: Human Resources Development Canada, 1997, p. 187).

13. Unless otherwise indicated, information for this section was taken from *Overview: Income Security Programs - Old Age Security, Canada Pension Plan* (Ottawa: Human Resources Development Canada, 1994), and from *Your Old Age Security Pension* (Ottawa: Human Resources Development Canada, 1996). Monthly benefit rates are for October to December 1997, as identified in *ISP - Information Card* (Ottawa: Human Resources Development Canada, 1997). The benefit amounts have been rounded to the nearest dollar.

14. Net income generally includes OAS payments, but these payments are not factored into the GIS reduction formula. Similarly, social assistance payments and CPP/QPP death benefits are not counted when calculating GIS eligibility.

15. *Annual Statistics on the Canada Pension Plan and Old Age Security* (Ottawa: Human Resources Development Canada, 1997, p. 187).

16. Unless otherwise indicated, information for this section was taken from: *Overview: Income Security Programs – Old Age Security, Canada Pension Plan* (Ottawa: Human Resources Development Canada, 1994); and, *Your Spouse's Allowance*.(Ottawa: Human Resources Development Canada, 1996). The various monthly benefit rates are for October to December 1997 as identified in *ISP - Information Card* (Ottawa: Human Resources Development Canada, 1997). The benefit amounts have been rounded to the nearest dollar.

17. The maximum SPA is reduced by 75 cents for every dollar of family income, until the OAS-equivalent portion disappears. Then, in the case of couples, both the GIS-equivalent portion of the SPA and the OAS pensioner's GIS are reduced by 25 cents for every dollar of combined income other than OAS. The GIS-equivalent portion of the SPA is reduced by 50 cents for every dollar in income other than OAS for widows/widowers.

18. *Annual Statistics on the Canada Pension Plan and Old Age Security* (Ottawa: Human Resources Development Canada, 1997, p. 187).

19. *A Pension Primer* (Ottawa: National Council of Welfare, 1996, pp. 13-14).

20. Information for this table was taken from provincial or territorial summaries compiled by the Social Program Information and Analysis Directorate, Social Policy Branch, Strategic Policy Group, at Human Resources Development Canada.

21. Unless otherwise stated, the information for this section was taken from the *General Income Tax Guide - 96* (Ottawa: Revenue Canada, 1997).

22. To calculate the maximum federal-provincial tax savings from the Age Credit, the Age Amount is multiplied by the federal tax credit rate of 17 per cent, plus provincial credits. The Age Amount in 1996 was $3,482. The average provincial tax rate in 1996 was 58 per cent of the federal rate, making the average joint federal-provincial tax credit rate approximately 27 per cent. Hence, the maximum Age Credit of $935 ($3,482 x .27). Note that the average provincial tax rate for 1997 is 54 per cent of the federal rate.

23. The Age Amount is reduced by 15 cents for each dollar in income above $25,921.

24. Residents of Quebec receive an Age Credit from their provincial government rather than from the federal government. In that province, the Age Amount used to calculate the Age Credit was $2,200, instead of the $3,482 used in the rest of Canada. As well, in 1996, the Age Amount in Quebec was reduced by only 7.5 cents for each dollar in income above $25,921. Starting in 1997, the reduction rate is the same as elsewhere in Canada – 15 cents for each dollar in income above $25,921.

25. "Private pension income" includes income from Registered Retirement Savings Plans (RRSPs), Registered Pension Plans (RPPs), and Deferred Profit Sharing Plans (DPSPs). Old Age Security benefits, Canada/Quebec Pension Plan benefits, and Saskatchewan Pension Plan benefits are not calculated as private pension income for the purposes of this credit.

26. To calculate the maximum federal-provincial tax savings from the Pension Income Credit, the Pension Income Amount is multiplied by the federal tax credit rate, plus provincial credits. The Pension Income Amount in 1996 was $1,000. Hence, the maximum Pension Income Credit of $270 ($1,000 x .27).

27. In Quebec, a parallel Pension Income Credit is delivered by the provincial government. It is also based on a $1,000 Pension Income Amount.

28. *Taxation Statistics on Individuals - Tax Year 1995* (Ottawa: Revenue Canada, 1997).

29. Calculations based on federal tax expenditure data in *Tax Expenditures - 1997* (Ottawa: Government of Canada, 1997, p. 28). The 1996 average provincial tax rate of 58 per cent was used to determine provincial costs.

30. Unless otherwise indicated, the information in this section was taken from *The Seniors Benefit - Securing our Future* (Ottawa: Government of Canada, 1996).

31. The choice of either moving to the new system or remaining with the current system would be based on the "family unit." In other words, one member of a couple could not choose to stay with the current system while the other chose the new system. Both must stay with the status quo or switch to new Seniors Benefit.

32. Unless otherwise indicated, information for this section was drawn from: Kenneth Bryden, *Old Age Pensions and Policy-making in Canada* (Montreal: McGill-Queen's University Press, 1974); David Ross, *The Working Poor* (Ottawa: Canadian Institute for Economic Policy, 1981); Dennis Guest, *The Emergence of Social Security in Canada* (Vancouver: University of British Columbia Press, 1985); and, Government of Canada, *Canada's Retirement Income Programs*, Statistics Canada,1996.

33. David Ross, *The Working Poor* (Ottawa: Canadian Institute for Economic Policy, 1981, pp. 34-37).

34. Ibid., p. 35.

35. *Improving the Canada Pension Plan* (Ottawa: National Council of Welfare, 1996, p. 6).

36. Unless otherwise indicated, the information for this section was drawn from: *Overview - Income Security Programs: Old Age Security, Canada Pension Plan.* (Ottawa: Human Resources Development Canada, 1994); *Retirement Pension - Canada Pension Plan* (Ottawa: Human Resources Development Canada, 1995); *Canada's Retirement Income Programs: A Statistical Overview* (Ottawa: Statistics Canada, 1996); and, *The Quebec Pension Plan* (Quebec: Régie des rentes du Québec, 1997). The monthly CPP/QPP benefit rates are for July to September 1997, as found in *ISP - Information Card* (Ottawa: Human Resources Development Canada, May 1997). Benefit amounts have been rounded to the nearest dollar.

37. All residents in Canada outside of Quebec and members of the Canadian Forces and the Royal Canadian Mounted Police contribute to the CPP, while residents of Quebec contribute to the QPP.

38. References in this chapter to the announced changes to the Canada Pension Plan were taken from *Securing the Canada Pension Plan: Agreement on Proposed Changes to the CPP* (Ottawa: Government of Canada, 1997). British Columbia and Saskatchewan were the only provinces that did not sign the 1997 agreement.

39. References in this chapter to the announced changes to the Quebec Pension Plan were taken from *Reforme du Régime de rentes du Quebec - Communiqué* (Québec: Régie des rentes du Québec, July 5, 1997). These and other QPP changes were verified with Régie officials.

40. The YBE and the YMPE are adjusted for inflation each January.

41. The difference between the 5.85 and 6 per cent contribution rates were captured when CPP contributors filed their 1997 taxes.

42. To calculate the combined CPP/QPP federal-provincial credit for someone paying the maximum contribution, the federal credit of 17 per cent, plus the 1996 provincial average of 58 per cent of the federal rate, were used. Hence, the combined credit is equal to 27 per cent of the maximum contribution ($969 x .27 = $262). For the self-employed, the CPP/QPP maximum contribution and credit are double that of a regular employee ($1,938 x .27 = $523).

43. *Information Card - ISP* (Ottawa: Human Resources Development Canada, May 1997).

44. QPP refers to this statement as a "Record of Contributions."

45. *Securing the Canada Pension Plan: Agreement on Proposed Changes to the CPP* (Ottawa: Government of Canada, 1997, p. 17).

46. *Annual Statistics on the Canada Pension Plan and Old Age Security* (Ottawa: Human Resources Development Canada, 1997, pp. 53 and 83).

47. *Le Régime de rentes du Québec, Statistiques 1996* (Québec: Régie des rentes du Québec, 1997, pp. 45-46). The number of beneficiaries refers to the number of people in receipt of QPP retirement benefits as of December 31, 1996. The Régie uses the month of December for their annual statistical comparisons. This applies to each instance where the number of QPP beneficiaries is used in this chapter.

48. Unless otherwise stated, information regarding CPP disability benefits was taken from *Disability Benefits: Canada Pension Plan* (Ottawa: Human Resources Development Canada, December 1994). Information regarding benefits under the QPP came primarily from *The Quebec Pension Plan* (Québec: Régie des rentes du Québec, 1997).

49.   Under the QPP, individuals who were eligible for disability benefits prior to
       January 1, 1994 receive the supplemental child's benefit until their dependant is
       25 years old, or until the year 2000, whichever comes first. Individuals eligible for
       QPP disability benefits after January 1st, 1994 are paid only the supplemental
       child's benefit until their dependant(s) reach(es) the age of 18.

50.   *Annual Statistics on the Canada Pension Plan and Old Age Security* (Ottawa:
       Human Resources Development Canada, 1997, pp. 53 and 83).

51.   *Le Régime de rentes du Québec, Statistics 1996* (Québec: Régie des rentes du
       Québec, 1997, pp. 45-46).

52.   *Annual Statistics on the Canada Pension Plan and Old Age Security* (Ottawa:
       Human Resources Development, 1997, pp. 53 and 83).

53.   *Le Régime de rentes du Québec, Statistics 1996* (Québec: Régie des rentes du
       Québec, 1997, pp. 45-46).

54.   *Annual Statistics on the Canada Pension Plan and Old Age Security* (Ottawa:
       Human Resources Development Canada, 1997, pp. 53 and 83).

55.   *Le Régime de rentes du Québec, Statistics 1996* (Québec: Régie des rentes du
       Québec, 1997, pp. 45-46).

56.   *Annual Statistics on the Canada Pension Plan and Old Age Security* (Ottawa:
       Human Resources Development Canada, 1997, p. 83).

57.   *Le Régime de rentes du Québec, Statistics 1996* (Québec: Régie des rentes du
       Québec, 1997, p. 46).

58.   *Annual Statistics on the Canada Pension Plan and Old Age Security* (Ottawa:
       Human Resources Development Canada, 1997, p. 53).

59.   *Le Régime de rentes du Québec, Statistics 1996* (Québec: Régie des rentes du
       Québec, 1997, pp. 45-46).

60.   Unless otherwise stated, the information for this section was taken from
       Canada's Retirement Income Programs: A Statistical Overview (Ottawa: Statistics
       Canada, 1996).

61.   Kenneth Bryden, *Old Age Pensions and Policy-Making in Canada* (Montreal:
       McGill-Queen's University Press, 1974, p. 38).

62.   Michael Prince, "Historical Analysis of Public Pension Schemes in Canada," in
       Reforming the Public Pension System in Canada: Retrospect and Prospect
       (Victoria, British Columbia: University of Victoria, p. 32).

63. *Budget Plan* (Ottawa: Government of Canada, 1996, p. 50).

64. The Saskatchewan Pension Plan (SPP) is an exception. It is a publicly administered, voluntary pension plan under the responsibility of the Saskatchewan Minister of Finance and available to residents of the province. The plan operates like other defined contribution or "money purchase" pension plans in Canada. For more information, contact the SPP at 1-800-667-7153.

65. Unless otherwise indicated, the information for this section came from *Pension Primer* (Ottawa: National Council on Welfare, 1996) and from *Canada's Retirement Income Programs: A Statistical Overview* (Ottawa: Statistics Canada, 1996).

66. The 1996 federal budget froze the annual Registered Pension Plan contribution limit at $13,500 until the year 2003. It is scheduled to rise to $14,500 in 2004 and to $15,500 in 2005.

67. Figures provided by the Pensions Section, Labour Division of Statistics Canada.

68. Calculations based on federal tax expenditure data in *Tax Expenditures - 1997* (Ottawa: Department of Finance Canada, 1997). The 1997 average provincial tax rate of 58 per cent was used to calculate the provincial costs.

69. Pension plans are able to comply with this provision without increasing their costs by providing an actuarially adjusted (reduced) retirement benefit.

70. Unless otherwise indicated, information for this section was taken from: *RRSPs and Other Registered Pension Plans for Retirement* (Ottawa: Revenue Canada, 1996); *Canada's Retirement Income Programs: A Statistical Overview* (Ottawa: Statistics Canada, 1996); and, *Pension Primer* (Ottawa: National Council on Welfare, 1996).

71. The 1996 federal budget froze the Registered Retirement Savings Plan contribution limit at $13,500 until the year 2003. It is scheduled to rise to $14,500 in 2004 and to $15,500 in 2005. See *Budget Plan* (Ottawa: Government of Canada, March 1996, p. 50). Note that these limits apply to individual contributors. Therefore, households with two spouses could contribute up to double the current maximum, or $27,000 a year.

72. The Pension Adjustment (PA) for contributory pension plans is simply the amount contributed to the plan in any given year. The PA for defined benefit plans, on the other hand, is the amount calculated as the annual benefit earned, similar to the concept of earned pension credits as in the Canada Pension Plan.

73. *Budget Plan* (Ottawa: Government of Canada, March 1996, p. 49).

74. Other financial institutions such as brokerage firms and investment dealers can also offer RRSPs by working through an authorized issuer, usually a trust company.

75. *Budget Plan* (Ottawa: Government of Canada, March 1996, p. 50).

76. Figures provided by the Pensions Section, Labour Division of Statistics Canada.

77. Calculations based on federal tax expenditure data in *Tax Expenditures - 1997* (Ottawa: Department of Finance Canada, 1997). The 1997 provincial tax rate of 58 per cent was used to calculate the provincial costs.

78. *Statistics on Individuals - 1994 Tax Year* (Ottawa: Statistics Canada, 1996).

79. Figures provided by the Pensions Section, Labour Division of Statistics Canada.

80. Figures provided by the Pensions Section, Labour Division of Statistics Canada.

81. Unless otherwise stated, the information for this section was taken from *Deferred Profit Sharing Plans - Information Circular [No.77-1R4]* (Ottawa: Revenue Canada, December 1992), and from *Canada's Retirement Income Programs: A Statistical Overview* (Ottawa: Statistics Canada, 1996).

82. *Budget Plan* (Ottawa: Government of Canada, March 1996, p. 50).

Chapter 5
The Distribution of Income Security Program Benefits

Introduction

For most Canadian households, private income provides the foundation of their economic security and well-being. Earnings from employment, investment returns, private pension benefits, and money from other market sources (including scholarships, bursaries, alimony, and severance pay) account for more than 85 per cent of Canadian households' total income.[1]

However, the benefits delivered through income security programs are also critical to the economic security and well-being of Canadians. These benefits protect individuals and families in the event of unforseen contingencies such as job loss, disability, or the death of a wage earner. They also provide assistance to people throughout the various stages of the life cycle, such as their child-raising and retirement years. And government benefits provide income support to those who, for a variety of reasons, cannot provide for themselves through the private market. Together, the various income security programs form Canada's "social safety net," filling in the gaps left by the private marketplace.

As demonstrated in the preceding chapters, Canada has a range of income security programs with different goals. These

115

programs can be divided into two general groups: those that insure earnings and those that provide basic income support. In addition, various government programs and tax provisions have been designed to meet particular social objectives such as recognizing, through child tax benefits, the costs and the value to society of raising children; mitigating the additional costs of living borne by persons with disabilities through credits and deductions in the income tax system; and, encouraging Canadians to save for their retirement through incentives such as Registered Retirement Savings Plans.

Programs that insure earnings are generally referred to as "social insurance" programs. The funds for these programs are raised through employer or employer/employee contributions – usually in the form of payroll deductions – and they are administered by governments. For example, Employment Insurance covers employees against a loss of earnings due to temporary unemployment, sickness, or parental leave. The Canada and Quebec Pension Plans protect workers and their dependants against lost earnings due to retirement, disability, or death. And provincial workers' compensation programs insure workers and their dependants against lost earnings due to workplace injury or death. Since social insurance programs are designed to protect the incomes of workers, and because the benefit levels of these programs are generally proportionate to earnings, middle-income households generally receive more from these programs than do low-income households.

Basic income support programs such as provincial social assistance and income-tested benefits through the old age security system are intended to provide a basic income for households, many of whom have little or no opportunity to earn money through private market sources. To the extent that provincial child benefits are now being used to replace portions of the welfare system, they too are increasingly taking on this basic income support role.[2] Unlike social insurance programs, basic income support programs are paid for out of general government revenues, and their benefits are usually targeted to low- and modest-income households.

Methodology

This chapter shows how the benefits of Canada's income security system are distributed among different income classes.[3] Drawing on data from Statistics Canada's *Survey of Consumer Finances*, the chapter examines the distribution of all benefits from income security programs received by the general population. It then highlights the program benefits that are received by the following groups:
• families with children
• working-age people
• senior citizens.

Throughout this chapter, information is presented for five income groups, also referred to as quintiles. These groups are divided according to their level of income before government transfers are taken into account (hereafter referred to as pre-transfer income).

For those unfamiliar with the concept of income quintiles, it is worthwhile describing it in more detail, since quintiles provide a very useful tool for understanding the distribution of income security program benefits. To create quintiles, households responding to Statistics Canada's income survey were ranked from the lowest to the highest on the basis of their annual pre-transfer income. Once ranked, the households were then divided into five groups, each containing an equal number of households. While the number of households in each quintile is the same, they differ significantly in terms of income. Those households in the first, or bottom, quintile have the *lowest* annual pre-transfer incomes, while those in the top quintile have the *highest* pre-transfer incomes. By dividing all of Canada's households into income quintiles, then looking at what proportion of income security benefits each group receives, it is possible to quickly characterize the distributive nature of income security programs.

The Distribution of Income Security Program Benefits

General Population

As one might expect, a large proportion of government transfers are received by households in the lower quintiles. This is shown in Table 14 which presents the distribution of pre-transfer incomes and government transfers among the various income groups.

Households in the two lowest quintiles have annual pre-transfer incomes of less than $23,000. These households receive only eight per cent of all pre-transfer income, but they collect nearly 64 per cent of all transfer income. By contrast, households in the two highest quintiles have annual pre-transfer incomes of more than $40,000. These households receive three-quarters of all pre-transfer income and only one-fifth of government transfers.

The clustering of government transfers among households at the low end of the income scale and the concentration of pre-transfer income at the top end appear most striking when households in the lowest and highest quintiles are compared. The lowest-income households receive less than one per cent of pre-transfer income, but nearly 40 per cent of all government transfers. By contrast, the highest-income households receive half of all pre-transfer income and just eight per cent of government transfers. Clearly, government income security programs reduce the degree of income inequality that results from pre-transfer income sources alone.

Table 14

Distribution of Pre-transfer Income and Government Transfers All Households, Canada, 1995				
Pre-transfer Income Groups (Quintiles)	Pre-transfer Annual Income Range ($)	Distribution of Pre-transfer Income (%)	Distribution of Government Transfers (%)	Distribution of Total Income (%)
lowest	less than 6,663	0.8	38.2	5.8
second	6,663 to 22,999	7.5	25.7	9.9
middle	23,000 to 40,361	16.1	16.2	16.1
fourth	40,362 to 63,999	26.1	12.0	24.2
highest	64,000 or higher	49.6	7.8	44.0
TOTAL		100.0	100.0	100.0

Source: Calculations by the Centre for International Statistics at the CCSD based on microdata from Statistics Canada's 1996 Survey of Consumer Finances.

To examine the impact of income security program benefits on household incomes, Table 15 shows average household incomes before and after government transfers. In 1995, the average annual pre-transfer household income was $39,235. This amount was supplemented by an average of $6,096 received in government transfer payments, raising the overall average household income to $45,331.[4]

Of course, not all households received $6,000 in transfer payments. On average, households in the bottom quintile received $11,658 in government transfers in 1995, while households in the top quintile received an average of $2,377 in transfer payments. As Table 15 shows, government transfers form a far greater proportion of annual income for the poorest households than for those in the higher quintiles. For households with the lowest pre-transfer incomes, government transfers represented nearly 90 per cent their annual income in 1995. Transfers also represented a substantial proportion of income for households in the second quintile: one-third of their total income came from government sources. By contrast, the highest-income households received less than three per cent of their total income from government transfers.

Table 15

Incomes Before and After Government Transfers All Households, Canada, 1995				
Pre-transfer Income Groups (Quintiles)	Average Pre-transfer Income ($)	Average Transfer Income ($)	Average Total Income After Transfers ($)	Transfer Income as % of Total Income
lowest	1,577	11,658	13,235	88.1
second	14,682	7,839	22,520	34.8
middle	31,502	4,932	36,435	13.5
fourth	51,318	3,681	54,999	6.7
highest	96,935	2,377	99,312	2.4
OVERALL AVERAGE	39,235	6,096	45,331	13.4

Source: Calculations by the Centre for International Statistics at the CCSD based on microdata from Statistics Canada's 1996 Survey of Consumer Finances.

Although the largest share of income transfers go to lower-income households, the benefits of these programs extend to middle- and higher-income households as well. That is because there are a variety of programs, each with its own roles and objectives. Some programs are meant to reduce poverty; others are designed as social insurance programs. Table16 shows the distribution of specific program benefits among income groups within the general population. For example, while social assistance benefits overwhelmingly go to households with the lowest pre-transfer incomes,[5] money from Employment

Insurance and the federal Child Tax Benefit is spread much more evenly across income groups.

The majority of Old Age Security and Canada/Quebec Pension Plan benefits go to households with low pre-transfer incomes. That is because most senior citizen households are in the lowest pre-transfer income quintiles. For these households, their non-government sources of income – mainly income from investments and private pension benefits – usually provide them with incomes well below the average incomes of households headed by people of working age.

Table 16

Distribution of Specific Transfer Benefits (%) All Households, Canada, 1995						
Pre-transfer Income Groups (Quintiles)	CTB	OAS	CPP/QPP	EI	SA	Other*
lowest	17.6	49.0	34.0	10.5	73.0	33.5
second	21.3	25.5	30.7	27.4	16.7	26.6
middle	26.7	12.5	16.8	23.4	5.6	18.9
fourth	24.5	7.9	11.7	22.2	2.9	10.9
highest	9.9	5.1	6.7	16.5	1.8	10.0
TOTAL	100.0	100.0	100.0	100.0	100.0	100.0

Source: Calculations by the Centre for International Statistics at the CCSD based on microdata from Statistics Canada's 1996 Survey of Consumer Finances.

* Examples of "other" transfer benefits include veterans' pensions and allowances (including widow and dependant benefits), workers' compensation benefits and training program benefits.

In Table 17, we can see the relative importance of the various income security programs as contributors to overall transfer income. The majority (51 per cent) of government transfer payments to households in 1995 were for Old Age Security and Canada/Quebec Pension Plan benefits. Employment Insurance accounted for about $1 of every $6 in transfer payments; social assistance accounted for just under $1 of every $7 in transfers; and payments for the Child Tax Benefit constituted the lowest proportion of transfers, accounting for less than one-tenth of all government income support expenditures.

The source of transfer income differed according to the income group. Social assistance income accounted for one-quarter of all transfer dollars going to households in the bottom quintile in 1995; it was second only to Old Age Security as a source of transfer income. For households in the middle quintile, the Canada and Quebec Pension Plans were the major sources of transfer dollars, followed by Employment Insurance. And for households in the top income quintile, the major source of transfer dollars was Employment Insurance benefits.

Table 17

Specific Transfer Benefits as a % of Total Transfer Income All Households, Canada, 1995							
Pre-transfer Income Groups (Quintiles)	CTB	OAS	CPP/QPP	EI	SA	Other	TOTAL
lowest	3.4	33.9	22.1	4.4	25.9	10.3	100.0
second	6.1	26.2	29.7	17.1	8.8	12.1	100.0
middle	12.2	20.4	25.8	23.2	4.7	13.7	100.0
fourth	15.0	17.4	24.1	29.6	3.2	10.6	100.0
highest	9.3	17.4	21.4	33.7	3.2	15.1	100.0
TOTAL (average)	7.4	26.4	24.9	16.0	13.6	11.7	100.0

Source: Calculations by the Centre for International Statistics at the CCSD based on microdata from Statistics Canada's 1996 Survey of Consumer Finances.

Families with Children

In this section, we examine the distribution of child tax benefits among families with children under 18 years of age, as well as the distribution of other transfers received by this group. Since families with children are generally headed by one or more working-age adults, their pre-transfer incomes tend to be higher than those of the population as a whole. As a result, when this group is separated into quintiles, higher thresholds for pre-transfer income result.

As is evident in Table 18, the majority of all transfer income received by families with children in 1995 went to households in the lower quintiles. Two-thirds of government transfers were paid to the poorest forty per cent of families, that is, families in the bottom two quintiles on the income scale. However, even with the government transfers, these families received only a small portion of the total income pie. For example, while the poorest families with children received 44 per cent of all transfer dollars in 1995, their share of total income was still only about six per cent. By contrast, the highest-income families with children received only seven per cent of all government transfers in 1995, but they held 40 per cent of total family income in Canada that year.

The poorest 20 per cent of families received roughly one-third of Child Tax Benefits in 1995, and the poorest 40 per cent of families (those with pre-transfer incomes of less than $37,600) received $6 of every $10 paid through the CTB program. The top income group – those with pre-transfer incomes of at least $75,500 – received only five per cent of the benefits paid through this program in 1995.

Table 18

Distribution of Child Tax Benefits, Total Transfers, and Total Income Families with Children under 18, Canada, 1995				
Pre-transfer Income Groups (Quintiles)	Pre-transfer Income Range ($)	Child Tax Benefit (%)	Total Transfers (%)	Total Income (%)
lowest	less than 18,164	32.1	44.3	6.4
second	18,164 to 37,599	28.8	23.3	12.4
middle	37,600 to 54,409	21.8	15.4	18.0
fourth	54,410 to 75,565	12.2	10.0	23.7
highest	75,566 or more	5.1	7.0	39.6
TOTAL		100.0	100.0	100.0

Source: Calculations by the Centre for International Statistics at the CCSD based on microdata from Statistics Canada's 1996 Survey of Consumer Finances.

Table 19

Child Tax Benefit as a % of Total Transfers and Total Income Families with Children, Canada, 1995		
Pre-transfer Income Groups (Quintiles)	Child Tax Benefit as a % of Total Transfers	Child Tax Benefit as a % of Total Income
lowest	19.4	12.6
second	33.1	5.8
middle	38.0	3.1
fourth	32.5	1.3
highest	19.8	0.3
OVERALL AVERAGE	26.8	2.5

Source: Calculations by the Centre for International Statistics at the CCSD based on microdata from Statistics Canada's 1996 Survey of Consumer Finances.

To examine how the CTB payments affect family income, and to gauge the size of these payments in relation to other transfer dollars received by families with children, Table 19 shows the CTB as a percentage of total family income and as a percentage of total transfers received. Among families with the lowest incomes in 1995, the CTB payments represented $1 out of every $8 of family income. While the CTB represents an important source of income for lower-income families with children, it constitutes only about one-fifth all government transfer dollars.

As pre-transfer income increases, the CTB represents a declining proportion of total family income. Among families in the middle-income quintile, for example, CTB payments make up three per cent of total family income. Although relatively small in relation to total family income, the CTB payments represent a significant share (38 per cent) of total transfer dollars received by these middle-income families.

The Working-age Population

In this section, we examine the distribution of income security benefits among all working-age households in the population, not just those with children under age 18. Working-age households are defined as those in which the head of the household (and the spouse, if applicable) are under 65 years of age. This group is the target for some of Canada's most important income security programs, including those related to earnings and social assistance. Because the working-age population excludes most retired persons, the incomes – and hence, the quintile thresholds – for this group are higher than for those of the general population. The pre-transfer income categories that divide working-age households into quintiles are shown in Table 20.

As Table 20 illustrates, there was a notable difference in the distribution of Employment Insurance and social assistance benefits among different income groups in 1995. As a social insurance program, EI provides temporary income support to eligible individuals who have paid premiums into the plan, and the benefits they receive are proportional to their earnings.[6]

Table 20

Distribution of Employment Insurance, Social Assistance Benefits, and Total Transfers and Income, Working-age Households, Canada, 1995					
Pre-transfer Income Groups (Quintiles)	Pre-transfer Income Range ($)	Employment Insurance (%)	Social Assistance (%)	Total Transfers (%)	Total Income (%)
lowest	less than 12,600	19.0	82.7	40.5	5.0
second	12,600 to 29,999	28.3	9.9	22.3	10.7
middle	30,000 to 46,396	19.7	3.6	15.2	16.9
fourth	46,397 to 69,609	18.9	2.3	13.1	24.7
highest	69,610 or more	14.1	1.6	8.9	42.8
TOTAL		100.0	100.0	100.0	100.0

Source: Calculations by the Centre for International Statistics at the CCSD based on microdata from Statistics Canada's 1996 Survey of Consumer Finances.

Because individuals are entitled to receive EI benefits regardless of their total family income, other workers in the household can still contribute their earnings to the family income. As a result, many middle- and upper-income households, as well as those in the lower quintiles, benefit considerably from Employment Insurance. By contrast, entitlement to social assistance is based on family income and it is targeted to households at the bottom of the pre-transfer income scale. Social assistance (commonly known as "welfare") is available only to households that have exhausted all other income options. The overwhelming proportion of social assistance benefits in 1995 were received by the poorest 20 per cent of working-age households.

Looking at the distribution of all government transfers – Employment Insurance, social assistance and other transfers – among working-age households, Table 20 shows that about 40 per cent of the transfers in 1995 went to those in the bottom income quintile (with pre-transfer incomes less than $12,600 per year), while roughly nine per cent of transfers went to households with pre-transfer incomes of $69,610 or more.

Table 21 shows that Employment Insurance accounted for a sizable portion of the total transfer dollars received by middle- and high-income working-age households in 1995. Even though EI did not contribute much to the total aggregate incomes of middle- and high-income earners, it remained an important income source for people who suffered a loss of employment. Social assistance was the most importance source of transfer dollars for working-age households at the low end of the income scale in 1995. It accounted for almost half of all government transfers received by this group, and nearly one-third of their total income.

Table 21

Employment Insurance and Social Assistance Benefits as a % of Total Transfers and Total Income Working-age Households, Canada, 1995				
Pre-transfer Income Groups (Quintiles)	Employment Insurance		Social Assistance	
	As a % of Transfers	As a % of Total Income	As a % of Transfers	As a % of Total Income
lowest	13.6	9.1	48.1	32.3
second	36.8	6.3	10.5	1.8
middle	37.6	2.8	5.5	0.4
fourth	41.8	1.8	4.1	0.2
highest	45.9	0.8	4.2	0.1
OVERALL AVERAGE	29.0	2.4	23.6	1.9

Source: Calculations by the Centre for International Statistics at the CCSD based on microdata from Statistics Canada's 1996 Survey of Consumer Finances.

Overall, Employment Insurance accounted for nearly one-third of all transfer dollars received by working-age households in 1995, while social assistance accounted for about one-quarter. The remaining transfer dollars received by working-age households came from a variety of programs including the CTB, Workers' Compensation, refundable tax credits, and the CPP/QPP (which included survivors', disability, and child benefits, as well as retirement benefits).

Senior Citizens

For Canada's senior citizens, government transfers are an extremely important source of income.[7] Because many seniors are fully or partially retired, they have little or no earnings from employment. Most of their pre-transfer income comes from investment returns and private pension plan benefits. As a result, the pre-transfer income ceilings or thresholds for quintiles of senior-citizen households are significantly lower than those of the general population (Table 22). Indeed, one-fifth of senior households in 1995 received less than $65 a year in pre-transfer income, and 80 per cent of these households had annual pre-transfer incomes of less than $28,836.

Unlike the distribution of government transfers among younger adult households – which is weighted towards the lower-income quintiles – the distribution of *total* government transfers is remarkably equal among senior citizens. In 1995, each quintile of senior households received about one-fifth of transfer payments.

However, a closer look at the distribution of benefits to senior citizens reveals some differences among the major transfer programs. The largest proportion of Old Age Security benefits go to lower-income senior households because the benefits are income-tested. At the same time, Canada/Quebec Pension Plan benefits tend to go more to middle- and higher-income senior households since these benefits are tied to working-life earnings and contributions.

Table 22

	Distribution of Old Age Security, Canada/Quebec Pension Plan Benefits and Total Transfers and Income, Senior Households, Canada, 1995				
Pre-transfer Income Groups (Quintiles)	Income Range ($)	Old Age Security (%)	Canada/ Quebec Pension Plan (%)	Total Transfers (%)	Total Income (%)
lowest	less than $65	24.9	14.1	20.4	9.1
second	65 to 5,179	22.0	17.7	20.5	10.6
middle	5,180 to 13,432	18.1	21.7	19.6	14.2
fourth	13,433 to 28,835	17.8	22.9	19.8	21.3
highest	28,836 or more	17.2	23.6	19.7	44.8
TOTAL		100.0	100.0	100.0	100.0

Source: Calculations by the Centre for International Statistics at the CCSD based on microdata from Statistics Canada's 1996 Survey of Consumer Finances.

Table 23 illustrates the relative importance of each of these transfer programs for senior citizens within the five income quintiles in 1995. Government transfers made up a sizable portion of the annual revenues for all groups of seniors, but the bottom quintile stands out: virtually *all* of the income for seniors in this group in 1995 came from Old Age Security benefits and the Canada/Quebec Pension Plans. Even seniors in the highest-income group counted on these programs for almost one-fifth of their total income in 1995.

Table 23

Old Age Security and Canada/Quebec Pension Plan Benefits as a Percentage of Transfer and Total Income Senior Households, Canada, 1995				
Pre-transfer Income Groups (Quintiles)	Old Age Security		Canada/Quebec Pension Plan	
	As a % of Transfers	As a % of Total Income	As a % of Transfers	As a % of Total Income
lowest	63.4	63.6	26.3	26.4
second	55.8	48.3	33.1	28.6
middle	48.1	29.6	42.3	26.1
fourth	46.7	19.5	44.2	18.5
highest	45.5	9.0	45.9	9.0
OVERALL AVERAGE	52.0	23.3	38.2	17.1

Source: Calculations by the Centre for International Statistics at the CCSD based on microdata from Statistics Canada's 1996 Survey of Consumer Finances.

Lower-income senior households rely most heavily on Old Age Security benefits, which accounted for almost two-thirds of all transfer dollars and total income for those in the bottom quintile in 1995. And, as indicated in Table 23, the proportion of total transfer dollars that came from the Canada/Quebec Pension Plan rose with household income.

Conclusion

While the overall distribution of government income security benefits is weighted towards Canada's poorest households, there are considerable variations in the distribution of particular program benefits among pre-transfer income groups. For example, social assistance benefits overwhelmingly go to the poorest 20 per cent of working-age households, but only about one-fifth of Employment Insurance benefits goes to those households. Unlike social assistance, Employment Insurance benefits are distributed fairly evenly among all quintiles of pre-transfer income earners. And among families raising children, the Child Tax Benefit is divided among a wide range of income-earners, with the poorest 40 per cent of families receiving the largest proportion and one-third of the benefits flowing to modest- and middle-income families.

The distribution patterns uncovered in this chapter also highlight the crucial role that income security programs play in keeping Canada's seniors out of severe poverty. Forty per cent of senior households receive less than $5,200 a year in pre-transfer income. For these people, approximately 85 per cent of their total income each year comes from Old Age Security and Canada/Quebec Pension Plan benefits. Only 20 per cent of senior-citizen households had pre-transfer incomes of more than $29,000 per year in 1995. Even for these households, OAS and CPP/QPP payments represented nearly one-fifth of their total incomes.

The presentation of incomes by quintiles, before and after government transfers (as seen in the preceding pages), shows that income security programs *do* redistribute income from the very highest to the very lowest pre-transfer income earners. But the remaining gap between high- and low-income earners remains large. The average income in the top quintile of households, including government transfers, was $99,000 in 1995; transfers accounted for only two per cent of their total income. The average income for the bottom quintile of households was $13,000 in 1995, with government transfers accounting for 88 per cent of their total income. In the end, the poorest 20 per cent of Canadian households received six per cent of all income in 1995, while the richest 20 per cent took home 44 per cent of total income.

Today's government-administered income security programs reflect decisions that have been made over the years to try to compensate for the market's inability to assure all Canadians of economic security. By presenting information about the distribution of income security program benefits among different income, age, and family groups, this chapter provides a backdrop for rational debate and discussion about the design and priorities of these government programs.

Endnotes

1. The analysis in this chapter was based on Statistics Canada's microdata file (Economic Families – 1995 Income) which contains data collected by the 1996 Survey of Consumer Finances. All computations on these microdata were done by the author, and the responsibility for the use and interpretation of these data is entirely that of the author.

    "Household" in this chapter includes what Statistics Canada refers to as "economic families" plus "unattached individuals." An "economic family" is defined by Statistics Canada as "a group of individuals sharing a common dwelling unit who are related by blood, marriage or adoption." An "unattached individual" is defined as "a person living alone or rooming in a household where he/she is not related to any other household members." These definitions are outlined in the *1996 Survey of Consumer Finances*.

2. See Chapter 1 for a discussion of recent child benefit policies.

3. This analysis considers only government transfer income and not in-kind benefits. The major components included in total transfer income are the following: the Child Tax Benefit; payments from Quebec Family Allowances and the Quebec Allowance for Newborn Children; Old Age Security, Guaranteed Income Supplement, and Spouse's Allowance payments; the Canada and Quebec Pension Plans; Employment Insurance; social assistance and other provincial income supplements; refundable provincial tax credits; and the Goods and Services Tax credit.

4. This chapter discusses the impact of government transfer programs. It does not consider the redistributive effects of income taxes or other taxes.

5. Some households with high pre-transfer incomes receive social assistance income, reflecting changes in the employment status of household members or changes in the household composition (such as a marriage or divorce) that may occur over the course of the year.

6.   See Chapter 3 for a discussion of EI benefits.

7.   Senior households are defined here as those where the head or spouse is aged 65 or older.

Glossary

This glossary is designed to explain and place into context various commonly used terms related to federal and provincial/territorial income security programs in Canada.

Benefit indexation: Automatic increases to a benefit based on changes in inflation. Changes in inflation are represented by changes in the Consumer Price Index or CPI (defined below). *Partial indexation* is when the indexation formula covers only a portion of the changes in inflation. Benefits for seniors, such as the Canada and Quebec Pension Plans and Old Age Security, provide full inflation protection because they are fully indexed to changes in inflation. The Child Tax Benefit, on the other hand, provides only partial inflation protection.

Block funding: Transfer of financial support from the federal government to the provinces/territories to pay for designated program areas. In some cases, block fund transfers may require that certain conditions be met in order for the province/territory to be eligible for the transfer dollars. The Canada Health and Social Transfer, or CHST (defined below), is an example of a block fund transfer. The CHST imposes several conditions on the provinces in the areas of health care and social assistance, but not in the field of post-secondary education.

Canada Health and Social Transfer (CHST): Federal transfer of cash and tax points ("tax points" defined below) to the provinces in support of health, post-secondary education, and social assistance and services. In 1996, the CHST replaced both the Canada Assistance Plan (CAP, 1966) – which transferred money to the provinces in support of social assistance and social services – and Established Programs Financing (EPF, 1977), which provided a combination of cash and tax points to support health and post-secondary education. CHST cash transfers are conditional upon the provinces upholding the five principles of the Canada Health Act and the principle of interprovincial mobility in the case of social assistance.

Claw-back: Reduction of an income benefit through the tax system. In 1989, the federal government introduced a "high-income claw-back" to Old Age Security (OAS) pension benefits and family allowances. In the case of OAS, the federal government taxed back some or all of the benefits paid to recipients whose personal income was above a particular income threshold. The claw-back on family allowances was based on the recipient's family income. The trend in the 1990s has been to introduce claw-backs into various programs which then tax back benefits at lower and lower income levels.

Consumer Price Index (CPI): Measure of changes in prices. The Consumer Price Index measures the retail prices of a "shopping basket" of about 300 goods and services, including food items, housing, transportation, clothing, and recreation. Not all items in the index are of equal "weight" or importance. For example, the index is more sensitive to price changes in housing than it is to price changes in entertainment. The CPI is used as an indicator of inflation in Canada. Changes in the CPI are said to reflect changes in the level of inflation or the "cost of living." The CPI is produced by Statistics Canada.

Cost-sharing: Financial arrangement whereby the federal government shares a percentage of the costs of designated programs administered by the provinces and territories. For example, under the Canada Assistance Plan, the federal government reimbursed the provinces for half (starting in 1990, less than half, in some cases) of their eligible expenditures on welfare and social services, provided that they met certain national standards.

Equalization: Cash payments from the federal government to the "have-not" (poorer) provinces to assist them in providing public services that are reasonably comparable in quality to those provided by the richer provinces, at reasonably comparable levels of taxation. The federal government uses a formula that measures each province's revenue-raising capacity against a five-province standard to determine which provinces are eligible for equalization payments, as well as the size of the payment. Currently, seven provinces qualify for equalization; only Ontario, Alberta, and British Columbia do not. Equalization is required under the Constitution.

Family income: For income tax purposes, the combined income of spouses. Family income does not include any income of children living at home.

Financial assistance: Cash support that either replaces or supplements income from employment and other sources. If a person's income from employment ceases due to retirement, unemployment, illness or disability, there are programs designed to provide *income support* – programs such as Old Age Security, the Canada and Quebec Pension Plans, Employment Insurance, Workers' Compensation, and social assistance. Other programs *supplement* one's existing income from work earnings or other sources; such programs include the Child Tax Benefit and provincial child benefits, the Guaranteed Income Supplement and provincial supplements for seniors. Financial assistance is usually in the form of a biweekly or monthly cheque.

Income-tested program: Program in which eligibility for benefits is determined by the applicant's level of family or individual income. An income ceiling or "threshold" establishes the level of income below which maximum benefits are paid. Benefits are reduced according to a pre-established "benefit reduction rate" when the individual or family income exceeds the income threshold. And an "income cut-off" establishes the level of individual or family income at which benefits cease to be paid. Since July 1996, it could be argued that the Old Age Security pension is an example of an income-tested program based on individual income. The Guaranteed Income Supplement for seniors, the Child Tax Benefit, and the proposed Seniors Benefit are examples of income-tested programs based on family income.

In-kind benefits: Non-cash benefits, also referred to as services. Examples include partially or fully subsidized child care, prescription drugs and dental coverage, training, and subsidized housing.

Means-tested program: Program in which eligibility for benefits is determined by the income and assets of an individual or family. There have been no pure means-tested programs in Canada since the mid-1960s when the Canada Assistance Plan replaced categorical assistance programs for the blind and persons with disabilities. The original federal Old Age Pension (which existed from 1927 until it was replaced by a universal pension plan in 1952) is an example of a means-tested benefit.

Needs-tested program: Program in which eligibility for assistance is based on the income, assets, and budgetary needs of an individual and their family. A "needs test" is used to determine eligibility for assistance. Under such a test, budgetary requirements are offset against income, and assistance is granted to cover any remaining deficit, within certain limits. Assets in excess of a certain fixed amount result in disentitlement. Certain assets may be exempt from the needs test, such as a primary house or car, within certain limits. Provincial social assistance or "welfare" is an example of a needs-tested program.

Net income: Total individual income from earnings, investments, and so on, minus allowable deductions such as Registered Pension Plan and Registered Savings Plan contributions, union dues, and child care expenses.

"Passive" versus "active" supports: *Passive* supports refer generally to assistance designed to provide income support, such as Employment Insurance income benefits or basic welfare assistance. *Active* supports refer broadly to measures designed to improve one's employability or support their participation in the workforce, such as support for child care, education and training, and self-employment start-up assistance.

Social insurance program: Program designed to protect or "insure" a portion of the earnings of individuals in the labour force against job loss, disability, illness, or retirement. Employment Insurance, Workers' Compensation, and the Canada and Quebec Pension Plans are examples of social insurance programs. While Employment Insurance and the Canada and Quebec Pension Plans are financed through mandatory contributions by individuals and employers, Workers' Compensation is supported solely through mandatory employer contributions. Benefits paid to individuals from these programs are tied to the individual recipient's level of earnings. In the case of EI and CPP/QPP, benefits also reflect an individual's contributions to the respective plans. One of the major functions of social insurance programs is to spread the risk of earnings loss across virtually the entire workforce.

Targeted program: Program in which benefits are paid primarily or entirely to individuals or families with low incomes. Provincial and territorial social assistance, the federal Guaranteed Income Supplement for seniors, and the Child Tax Benefit are commonly referred to as targeted programs because they are designed to *target* benefits to individuals and families with very low incomes, that is, to those most "in need."

Tax credit: Provision which reduces taxes that would otherwise be payable by an individual taxpayer. Tax credits can be either *refundable* or *non-refundable*. For those with taxable income, *refundable tax credits* reduce the amount of taxes owed. Those without taxable income – or taxes payable – receive a cheque from the government for the amount of the credit. *Non-refundable tax credits*, on the other hand, only reduce the amount of taxes owed, therefore, persons who have no taxable income derive no benefit from such credits. The Equivalent-to-Spouse Credit and the Age Credit are examples of non-refundable credits, while the GST Credit is an example of a refundable credit.

Tax deduction: Provision that allows tax filers to subtract the value of eligible expenses from their taxable income, up to certain limits. Examples include the deduction of various business expenses by self-employed persons, the Registered Retirement Savings Plan and Registered Pension Plan tax deduction, and the Child Care Expense Deduction.

Tax exemption: Provision which allows a certain amount of income not to be subject to tax. The tax exemption for families with children that was in place from 1919 until the mid-1980s is an example of a tax exemption. Today, tax exemptions are less common than either tax deductions or tax credits in the personal income tax system.

Tax expenditure: General term which refers to the range of provisions that reduce one's taxable income such as tax credits, deductions, and exemptions. These provisions are commonly used to achieve certain social or economic objectives, such as improving the incomes of individuals or families, or offsetting particular personal costs through the income tax system. The use of the word "expenditure" reflects the fact that these provisions impose a cost on governments in that they represent foregone tax revenues.

Tax points: Term which refers to the estimated value of "tax room" transferred from the federal to the provincial governments. As part of the Established Programs Financing arrangement of 1977, the federal government reduced its corporate and personal tax rates, thus allowing the provinces to increase their own rates to fill in this newly vacated tax room. This additional tax room was used to replace the cost-shared cash transfer arrangements for health and post-secondary education that were in place at the time. When the EPF was rolled into the CHST in 1996, the CHST absorbed the transferred tax room, the value of which the federal government calculates as tax points.

Territorial Formula Financing: Financial arrangement under which the federal government provides cash transfers to the territorial governments in support of public services. The transferred funds are provided without federal conditions about how the money is spent. The amounts transferred are based on a formula that takes into account both the expenditure requirements and the revenue capacity of the receiving jurisdictions.

Transfers: There are two basic types of transfers – transfers *between governments* and transfers from governments *to individuals*. Transfers *between governments* are financial arrangements whereby one level of government gives (or "transfers") financial assistance to another level of government to fund a particular activity or set of activities. The Canada Health and Social Transfer, Equalization, and Territorial Formula Financing are examples of transfers between levels of government. Transfers *to individuals*, on the other hand, include the full range of income security programs which provide income benefits, such as Employment Insurance, the Canada and Quebec Pension Plans, child benefits, and so on.

Universal program: Program that provides benefits to all citizens or to those within a particular demographic group, such as families with children or the elderly, regardless of their income. Also referred to as a "demogrant" program. Old Age Security benefits and family allowances were universal programs until 1989, at which time the government began taxing back benefits from higher-income recipients. Today, income security programs are not generally universal, but there are some exceptions such as the Veterans Disability Pension which is paid to all eligible veterans, regardless of their financial situation.

Appendix 1

Changes in 1998

As noted in the Introduction, several changes had just taken place or were announced as this book went to print in early 1998. The following section summarizes these changes, including those outlined in the 1998 federal budget.

Employment Insurance Contribution and Benefit Rates

Effective January 1998, the employee contribution rate for Employment Insurance dropped from $2.90 per $100 of insurable earnings to $2.70, while the employer contribution rate fell from $4.06 per $100 to $3.78. The maximum benefit rates in 1998 are unchanged from those of 1997.

Canada and Quebec Pension Plan Contribution Rates

The combined employer-employee contribution rate for both the Canada and Quebec Pension Plans rose from 6.0 per cent of pensionable earnings to 6.4 per cent, effective January 1998. The new rate applies throughout the 1998 calendar year. At the same time, the maximum pensionable earnings for CPP/QPP rises from $35,800 to $36,900. With this increase in the contribution rate and in the maximum insurable earnings, the maximum annual CPP/QPP employer-employee contribution rises from $1,938 in 1997 to $2,138 in 1998. This amount is split equally between employees and their employers. Self-employed workers are responsible for the full contribution amount.

Canada and Quebec Pension Plan Benefit Rates, 1998		
Type of Benefit	Canada Pension Plan 1998 Maximum Monthly ($)	Quebec Pension Plan 1998 Maximum Monthly ($)
Retirement (at age 65)	745	751
Disability	895	900
Disability child supplement	170	54
Survivor (under age 65)	411	411
Survivor (age 65 and older)	447	450
Orphan	170	54
Survivor/Retirement	745	751
Survivor/Disability	895	1,087

Old Age Security Benefits

Old Age Security Benefits are adjusted quarterly, based on changes in the Consumer Price Index. They are reviewed each January, April, July, and October. Contact Human Resources Development Canada for the latest rates. Due to low inflation in recent years, quarterly adjustments have been very small.

Changes Announced in the 1998 Federal Budget

Seniors Benefit
Legislation for the proposed Seniors Benefit is expected to be tabled at some point in 1998. In the budget, the federal government stated that it is "currently reviewing the details of

the proposal in light of the valuable suggestions received during [the] consultations" – a reference to public and private consultations about the Seniors Benefit held by the government in 1997. It is expected that changes will be made to the proposed package described in Chapter 4.

Canada Child Tax Benefit
The federal government will increase spending on the Canada Child Tax Benefit by $425 million in July 1999, and by another $425 million in July 2000. Details on how this new money will affect benefit levels are to be announced in the 1999 federal budget.

Caregiver Tax Credit
A new Caregiver Tax Credit will be available to individuals who care for elderly family members or dependent relatives with infirmities. This credit is designed to provide support to families that care for an elderly parent or grandparent but do not qualify for tax assistance because the dependant's income from the Old Age Security pension and the Guaranteed Income Supplement exceeds the income threshold of $6,456 per year under the existing Infirm Dependant Credit.

The new credit will reduce a claimant's federal taxes owed by up to $400 a year. The credit will be reduced by the amount that the dependant's net income exceeds $11,500, and it will disappear once their net income reaches $13,853. The Caregiver Tax Credit is expected to provide about $120 million annually in new tax assistance to about 450,000 caregivers.

Child Care Expense Deduction
The expense limits for the Child Care Expense Deduction will be increased from $5,000 to $7,000 for children under the age of seven or for dependants for whom a disability tax credit has been claimed. The limits will rise from $3,000 to $4,000 for children between the ages of 7 and 16 or for dependants who are not eligible for the $7,000 deduction, but who have a mental or physical infirmity. These measures are expected to provide

an additional $45 million in tax assistance to about 65,000 families.

Employment Insurance Premiums on Behalf of Youth
Employers will be exempt from paying Employment Insurance premiums (or contributions) for employees hired in 1999 and 2000 who are between the ages of 18 and 24 years.

Income Tax Changes

The information in this book regarding various tax provisions – such as tax credits and deductions – was based on the 1996 taxation year. Only a few of the income tax changes for the 1997 taxation year were relevant to the contents of this book, and they are noted within the chapters, in sections describing the various tax provisions.

Appendix 2

Number of Weeks of Entitlement for EI Benefits

Unemployment Rate in Claimant's Region

Hours of work	6% and under	over 6% to 7%	over 7% to 8%	over 8% to 9%	over 9% to 10%	over 10% to 11%	over 11% to 12%	over 12% to 13%	over 13% to 14%	over 14% to 15%	over 15% to 16%	over 16%
420-454									26	28	30	32
455-489								24	26	28	30	32
490-524							23	25	27	29	31	33
525-559						21	23	25	27	29	31	33
560-594					20	22	24	26	28	30	32	34
595-629				18	20	22	24	26	28	30	32	34
630-664			17	19	21	23	25	27	29	31	33	35
665-699		15	17	19	21	23	25	27	29	31	33	35
700-734	14	16	18	20	22	24	26	28	30	32	34	36
735-769	14	16	18	20	22	24	26	28	30	32	34	36
770-804	15	17	19	21	23	25	27	29	31	33	35	37
805-839	15	17	19	21	23	25	27	29	32	34	36	38
840-874	16	18	20	22	24	26	28	30	32	34	36	38
875-909	16	18	20	22	24	26	28	30	32	34	36	38
910-944	17	19	21	23	25	27	29	31	33	35	37	39
945-979	17	19	21	23	25	27	29	31	33	35	37	39
980-1014	18	20	22	24	26	28	30	32	34	36	38	40
1015-1049	18	20	22	24	26	28	30	32	34	36	38	40
1050-1084	19	21	23	25	27	29	31	33	35	37	39	41
1085-1119	19	21	23	25	27	29	31	33	35	37	39	41
1120-1154	20	22	24	26	28	30	32	34	36	38	40	42
1155-1189	20	22	24	26	28	30	32	34	36	38	40	42
1190-1224	21	23	25	27	29	31	33	35	37	39	41	43
1225-1259	21	23	25	27	29	31	33	35	37	39	41	43
1260-1294	22	24	26	28	30	32	34	36	38	40	42	44
1295-1329	22	24	26	28	30	32	34	36	38	40	42	44
1330-1364	23	25	27	29	31	33	35	37	39	41	43	45
1365-1399	23	25	27	29	31	33	35	37	39	41	43	45
1400-1434	24	26	28	30	32	34	36	38	40	42	44	45

continued on next page

Unemployment Rate in Claimant's Region

(continued from previous page)

Hours of work	6% and under	over 6% to 7%	over 7% to 8%	over 8% to 9%	over 9% to 10%	over 10% to 11%	over 11% to 12%	over 12% to 13%	over 13% to 14%	over 14% to 15%	over 15% to 16%	over 16%
1435-1469	25	27	29	31	33	35	37	39	41	43	45	45
1470-1504	26	28	30	32	34	36	38	40	42	44	45	45
1505-1539	27	29	31	33	35	37	39	41	43	45	45	45
1540-1574	28	30	32	34	36	38	40	42	44	45	45	45
1575-1609	29	31	33	35	37	39	41	43	45	45	45	45
1610-1644	30	32	34	36	38	40	42	44	45	45	45	45
1645-1679	31	33	35	37	39	41	43	45	45	45	45	45
1680-1714	32	34	36	38	40	42	44	45	45	45	45	45
1715-1749	33	35	37	39	41	43	45	45	45	45	45	45
1750-1784	34	36	38	40	42	44	45	45	45	45	45	45
1785-1819	35	37	39	41	43	45	45	45	45	45	45	45
1820-	36	38	40	42	44	45	45	45	45	45	45	45

Source: Human Resources Development Canada. *Employment Insurance: Regular Benefits,* 1997, pp. 8-9.